HM
133
H95
1980

Hyman, Herbert
The psycho...

DATE DUE

+HM133 .H95 1980

THE PSYCHOLOGY OF STATUS

This is a volume in the Arno Press collection

DISSERTATIONS ON SOCIOLOGY

Advisory Editors
Harriet Zuckerman
Robert K. Merton

See last pages of this volume for a complete list of titles

THE PSYCHOLOGY OF STATUS

Herbert Hiram Hyman

ARNO PRESS
A New York Times Company
New York • 1980

26692

Editorial Supervision: Doris Krone

First Publication 1980 by Arno Press Inc.
Copyright © 1980 by Herbert Hiram Hyman
Printed by permission of Herbert Hiram Hyman
DISSERTATIONS ON SOCIOLOGY
ISBN for complete set: 0-405-12945-9
See last pages of this volume for titles.
Manufactured in the United States of America

Library of Congress Cataloging in Publication Data

Hyman, Herber Hiram.
   The psychology of status.

   (Dissertations in sociology)
   Reprint of the 1942 ed. published by Columbia University, New York, which was issued as no. 269 of Archives of psychology.
   Bibliography; p.
   1. Reference groups. 2. Social status.
I. Title. II. Series. III. Series: Archives of psychology ; no. 269.
HM133.H95   1980   305   79-9005
ISBN 0-405-12974-2

The Psychology of Status

BY
HERBERT HIRAM HYMAN, Ph.D.

ARCHIVES OF PSYCHOLOGY
R. S. WOODWORTH, Editor
No. 269

NEW YORK
June, 1942

ACKNOWLEDGMENTS

The writer wishes to express his gratitude to Professor Otto Klineberg and Dr. John Volkmann for their sustained interest, generous advice, and supervision of the study; to Professor H. E. Garrett for kindly suggestions as to the statistical treatment of the data; to Professor Hadley Cantril who graciously allowed the writer to use his unpublished materials; to Miss Rosalea Schonbar and Mr. Harold Proshansky who aided in the drawing and construction of the figures and chart; to Mr. Robert Chin for helping with the data; and to all the friends, particularly Mr. Israel Zwerling, who cooperated in securing subjects.

In addition the writer would like to express his deep appreciation to his family who made possible this study.

CONTENTS

CHAPTER		PAGE
I.	INTRODUCTION	5
II.	THE INTERVIEW APPROACH TO SUBJECTIVE STATUS	13
III.	THE CONSTRUCTION OF A RELIABLE SCALE FOR THE MEASUREMENT OF STATUS	39
IV.	THE RELATION OF THE REFERENCE GROUP TO JUDGMENTS OF STATUS	47
V.	THE COMPOSITION OF GENERAL STATUS WITH REFERENCE TO THE ROLE OF VALUES	58
VI.	STATUS AND ATTITUDES	67
VII.	IMPLICATIONS AND SUGGESTIONS FOR THE FUTURE	80
	SUMMARY AND CONCLUSIONS	90
	BIBLIOGRAPHY	92

CHAPTER I

INTRODUCTION

The concept of status has been of interest to psychologists, since status may be thought to produce or correspond with certain predictable attitudes of the individual. Status also corresponds with aspects of behavior, by definition, since role and status are inseparable (46). It affects one's social perspective because people in different positions in society will have different views of social change. Status is also an integral part of social organization, and any understanding of the relation of "culture and personality" demands analysis of status.

The term status has been defined in a variety of ways. It may be used in the legal sense as the sum of the legal capacities of an individual (63), or to refer solely to economic position (21), or to the totality of positions of a person (64) or to refer only to a fixed position in an hierarchical social order (69). Most definitions of status imply that it is the position of an individual relative to other individuals. Status will be so defined in this study. The term, however, will not be limited to a particular kind of position. Within a society there are many specific patterns or structures in which a person may occupy a position. Each individual, consequently, has many statuses corresponding to the number of patterns in which he participates, *e.g.*, economic and social. Each such position within a specific pattern may be called a status. The term, however, may also refer to some complex of all such specific positions or statuses. In this latter case, the concept may be denoted as general status.

Most determinations of status have in the past been made on the basis of some *objective* criterion such as income, or some institutional feature such as membership in a given occupational group or caste. In this study it is proposed to deal with an area of status which may be called "subjective status" (as contrasted with the above objective status) which may be defined as a person's conception of his own position relative to other individuals. The term subjective is not associated in this study with the connotations unverifiable or unreliable. The reliability of measures of subjective status will be dealt with later. The word refers only to the dependence of the measure upon the subject's report.

An adequate knowledge of behavior and attitudes can come only through analysis of both objective and subjective status. The usefulness of measures of objective status is not denied. Sociologists, economists, and anthropologists have important reasons for using such measures. For example, economists get insight into the degree of actual stratification in our society; ethnologists like Linton (45) seek an understanding of society by reference to the categories in which people are classified. Status systems may be regarded as such modes of classification. Objective status, as well, may be an important consideration for psychologists. For example, Kornhauser (38) discusses the consequence of membership in a given objective economic class (class could be identified with the group of persons in the same economic status). He points out that members of given status groups have predictable psychological characteristics as a function of two factors: 1. The individual can be expected to show certain characteristics as a result of objective class membership since the objective conditions for membership such as income will define and delimit the range of satisfaction for needs. For example, within the low income groups, only some needs can be satisfied while other needs cannot, and this may apply to biological needs as well as cultural wants. 2. People of a given economic status might show psychological characteristics as a function of selection. People in the $10,000 income group might be the ones who got there by virtue of aggressiveness or conservatism.

The intent of the following discussion is to show the necessity of distinguishing between objective and subjective status. There is no intent, however, to minimize the importance of objective status as a variable correlated with subjective status or as a variable that partially determines subjective status.

Two possible reasons for the neglect of subjective status may be offered: 1. This private area of status may not have been considered at all. 2. It may have been assumed that the objective status coincides with the person's conception of his own position. The fact that the two areas do not coincide is demonstrated by a number of studies reported below. The difference between the two measures is a function of two factors: 1. A person may be aware of his objective status, but a different subjective status may be a mode of adjustment to an unpleasant objective status. A study of the discrepancy between these two statuses might be an approach to the psychology of adjustment. 2. The individual may not be aware of his objective status at all. Subjective status, consequently, may not represent an adjustment to a recognized objective status. It may be that people arrive at their view of status by reference to criteria that the psychologist or sociologist has omitted in his analysis. It might be naive, for example, to expect that people reckon their status by the number of daily papers they receive, which has been used as an item included in the index of status. When the ethnologist reconstructs the social organization of a society, he does so mainly from the reports of informants and the observation of the behavior of individuals. Hence, the only way to find out the criteria for status is by an actual field study of the way people view the matter of status. This method approximates the definition of subjective status with one qualification: Such studies might be of two kinds—the way people view the status of others, and the way people view their *own* status. It is with this latter area that the study deals.

There are, consequently, three sets of operations by which status may be measured: 1. Determination on the basis of objective criteria. 2. Determination of an individual's status by reference to his conception of his own position. 3. Determination of an individual's status in accordance with the way other people view it. The corresponding terms used to refer to these three sets of operations are, respectively, *objective* status, *subjective* status, and *accorded* status.

LITERATURE

Suggestions of the distinction between objective and subjective status may be found in various sources. Allport (2) states that the psychologist often interprets a subject's behavior in terms of his own frame of reference instead of the subject's frame of reference. Such would be the case when objective and subjective status are confused. Hartmann (27) states that "'Status' and 'prestige' have only psychological reality, but they are intangible existences which are founded upon objective phenomena and lead to genuine modifications of behavior." He argues that the Sims and other scales of socio-economic status which use objective indices yield only rough classifications of status.

Cantril (11) states that, "To an outside observer there may be an enormous discrepancy between the status an individual assigns himself and the objective criteria a person exhibits to qualify in that status. Thus in selecting respondents in the proper proportion according to their economic status, experts who poll public opinion realize that an aristocratic old man who carries a cane, who once possessed a fortune but now is poverty-stricken and lives in a garret will still identify himself with the upper class and have all the opinions characteristically held by the wealthy."

Roper (67) recognizes the inadequacy of certain objective measures of economic status such as income although he does not discuss subjective status. He mentions the variable of "reference group" by indicating the fact that two people of equal income living in different areas may have different relative statuses depending on the incomes of their associates. (This variable of reference group will be systematically dealt with in Chapter III.) Roper's sampling takes into account the relativity of economic status to the reference group. His prosperous group includes those able to afford the luxuries common to *their community*. Wilks (83) discusses the inadequacy of criteria such as income in the determination of representative samples of economic classes. He also indicates that the meaning of a given income as a criterion for the determination of economic status is relative to the geographical area. He deals with this reference group problem by sampling in a way similar to Roper.

A recognition of the importance of subjective status can be noted in several of the *Fortune* polls (62, 78). Katz and Cantril (35) in discussing the *Fortune* poll for the 1936 presidential election designate it a "psychological poll." The interviewer was instructed to select his cases in accordance with psychological identifications and objective status. The actual income was less important than the income group with which the subject identified himself and with which he was identified by the community. This was a practical recognition of the psychological fact that a person's ideas and actions may be more closely related to his subjective rather than his objective status. They cite examples of this tendency such as the following: A one time aristocrat may have aristocratic attitudes despite the fact that he no longer has a butler and country home: an individual who derives 5% of his income from investments and 95% of his income from work may still identify himself with capital.

Similar validation of the discrepancy between subjective and objective status is seen in the *Fortune* poll of February, 1940, in which 79.2% of the American population identified themselves with the middle class, 7.6% with the upper, and 7.9% with the lower class. It may be argued that this response represents a reaction to the highly valent term "lower class" or "upper class" and is indicative of the emotional recoil from the term rather than true identification with middle class status. It seems to the writer that this is not an adequate critique of the results. It is true that one could theoretically make a dichotomy between an intellectual or realistic class identification and one involving emotional recoil from the valent term, class. Probably, one could minimize the degree of emotionality by rephrasing the terms in the *Fortune* study. Yet practically, the operations of subjective status are rarely devoid of affective features as will be indicated in the interview data in Chapter II. Class identification and the departure of subjective from objective status may be a function of just such emotional factors. Also, it might be a spurious representation of the life situation if the *Fortune* study were phrased without emotional terms, since differences in status are continually reinforced in social relations by differential rewards, invidious comparisons, opprobrium, or prestige. The amount of such emotional recoil in the study from the term lower class indicates the potency of the factors by which members of an objectively low class may diverge subjectively from an unpleasant low status.

Holcombe (31) specifically mentions the importance of subjective status. He states, "Classes may be defined by economists in terms of property, income, or position in the economic order. Such objective classifications possess indubitable utility in economic analysis. But politicians need classifications which are subjective as well as objective, for they wish to know not only how voters stand in the economic order, but also how they think and feel and are likely to act." This view suggests the primacy of subjective status over objective status in the determination of attitudes and behavior. In discussing the results of the *Fortune* poll, Holcombe says that "not one in a dozen thinks of himself as a proletarian." If this is true, it would presumably be hard to find a correspondence between low objective status and "low-class" attitudes.

Cantril (12) has extensive data on subjective class-identification for a representative sample of the total population.[1] The subjects answered the two questions: "What income group in our country do you feel that you are a member of—the middle income group, the upper income group, or the lower income group?" "To what social class in this country do you feel you belong—middle class, upper, or lower?" Data on objective status (income and interviewer estimate) were recorded and attitudes on social issues were broken down according to objective and subjective class. (These materials will be dealt with in later portions of the paper.) The data are superior to the *Fortune* poll in one respect. The *Fortune*

---

[1] The author wishes to express his gratitude to Professor Hadley Cantril for permission to use his unpublished materials.

questions did not designate the kind of class. Consequently, the dimension of status judged by all subjects may not have been the same. Some individuals may have identified on the basis of social class, others on the basis of economic class, and there is no knowledge as to what kind of status the data refer. In this study the aspect of status to be judged was clearly specified as social or economic. The results approximate the *Fortune* poll and again indicate the large discrepancy between objective and subjective status. Seventy-one and seven-tenths percent of the population identified themselves with the middle economic classes, 1.4% with the upper class, and 26.9% with the lower class. The analogous figures for social class are—87.4% middle class, 4.9% upper class, and 7.7% lower class.

The American Institute of Public Opinion for April 2, 1939, reports (4) similar data on the discrepancy between subjective class-identification and objective status. Eighty-eight percent of the subjects identified with the middle class, and six percent each with the upper and lower classes respectively.

Hartmann and Newcomb (28) suggest certain subjective factors in status. They state that economic class identification may be on the basis of "levels of aspiration," ideas, or standards which make the values of one economic group more impressive than those of another. They say that subjective patterns of reactions (attitudes) are imperfectly correlated with the objective division of wealth in the population.

A variety of other approaches to the measurement of status may be mentioned. Certain measures related to *accorded status* have been reported. For example, Zeleny (85) thinks the status of a person is what others think of him. The index stripped of statistical sophistication is really the sociometric one of the summation of positive preferences for a person. Hunt and Solomon (32), and Newstetter, Feldstein, and Newcomb (60) use essentially the same sort of index. While these operations are apparently those of accorded status, nothing can be inferred from the measures about the relative position of individuals. The assumption of these measures, it seems to the writer, is that preference for a given individual implies that he has a certain accorded status. The subjects, however, are not asked what the status of another person is. They are asked if they prefer him for a bunkmate or classmate. Individuals may be preferred because they are of high status and offer vicarious status, or because they are of low status and can be dominated. Furthermore, the measure is essentially concerned with affectivity and does not elucidate status in relation to economic or other patterns of social organization. Nor does the measure imply a determinate objective status. Lundberg (47) found that 60% of the sociometric choices by people were to individuals of higher socioeconomic status. Consequently, attraction between people does not imply equality of status. In 60% of the cases it implies a superordinate-subordinate status situation, and the other 40% of the choices are indeterminate. While the index has these limitations, it may yield interesting data. (The reader is referred to the above references.)

For a review of objective measures of status the reader is referred to McCormick (52) and Kerr and Remmers (37). These measures use such indices of status as occupation, possession of a telephone, material possessions in the home, rent, daily papers received, presence of electric light, quality of neighborhood, etc.

Ethnological treatments of status offer valuable comparative material on the way status is structured in different societies and the relations of status to many variables of social organization and behavior. These treatments really use the operations of both objective and accorded status. Status is determined by reference to three classes of objective factors: 1. Personal factors such as age, sex, health, and size. 2. Participational factors such as degree of control over property, religious, economic, or military activity. 3. Membership in given groups such as voluntary associations, family, castes, or class groups. However, the method of investigation probably proceeds at first by accorded status. The ethnologist through reports of informants must elicit the status of individuals, and then determine the relation of the above classes of factors to a given status. The reader is referred to Linton (46), Mead (54), Mishkin (56), and Richardson (65).

The Investigation of Subjective Status

A research program in the field falls into two parts: A. A study of the nature of people's views of their own status. This study can be approached in part through the avenue of the Psychology of judgment, since the individual can be asked to make a judgment of his own position relative to others. A judgmental approach has two important consequences. The results may extend the generality of principles of judgment to new materials of a "social" nature. More important, within this methodological framework, we already have at our disposal certain leads as to what are the variables that determine subjective status, by reference to the variables that determine the properties of judgments in general. B. A study of the relation of subjective status to social attitudes and other dependent variables. This aspect of the program will be limited to a study of radical attitudes. Of necessity the first area will be the major one dealt with since we have to know the properties of subjective status before we can determine the functional relationships demanded by the second problem.

Two procedures were used in the investigation of the nature of subjective status: 1. *Controlled interview:* Since the area is relatively unknown, it was decided to do a series of intensive interviews on a heterogeneous population in an attempt to obtain suggestions as to the kind of experimental work to be done, and to obtain information about aspects of the problem not readily amenable to experimental study. 2. *Experimental studies:* On the basis of the interview materials, three experiments were devised which demonstrate more conclusively certain results suggested in the interviews.

Since the entire study represents one of the first ventures into a new field, its chief value will be exploratory rather than definitive.

CHAPTER II

THE INTERVIEW APPROACH TO SUBJECTIVE STATUS

The interview findings indicate a variety of trends in the operation of certain independent variables in subjective status. Findings are also reported on emotional accompaniments, genesis of status, and allied problems. A fairly heterogeneous population was used in this study. No claim is made for the representativeness of the sample. It was not practicable for a single interviewer to interview large numbers of subjects in various geographical areas or at all status levels in the total population. The results of the interviews are consequently not intended to be definitive, but the generality of the processes involved in subjective status and the action of certain of the variables demonstrated are assumed to extend beyond the population sampled.

Subjects

All subjects used were adults with relative independence of economic status, *i.e.*, all male subjects were working for their own livelihood, female subjects were either working or married, and in most cases, the subjects lived in separate households from their parents. It was felt that students, children, or other individuals who were living with their parents, would have equivocal status and would represent too complex a status picture for an introductory study. Thirty-one subjects were used, thirteen men and eighteen women. Thirteen were married, sixteen single, and two were widowed. Twenty had college degrees or higher or were at present studying in college. Twelve of the subjects were Christian, 19 Jewish. The incomes ranged from $336 to $6100 a year. The income distribution is presented below.

TABLE 1
INCOMES OF THE SUBJECTS

Income	Frequency	Income	Frequency
0– 499	1	3000–3499	1
500– 999	6	3500–3999	1
1000–1499	9	4000–4499	1
1500–1999	2	4500–4999	2
2000–2499	4	5000–6000	0
2500–2999	3	6000–plus	1

The occupations that were represented include doctors, nurses, college teachers, students, clerks, salesmen, editors, housewives, waitresses, managers, engineers, and domestic workers. All of the subjects were drawn from an urban population. The sampling should be broadened to include rural people, other geographical areas, and people of other occupations.

Procedure

The interviews lasted approximately two hours per subject. They were relatively intense "clinical" examinations. The questions were not standardized in their presentation. It was thought that complete standardization would not permit sufficient modification of the questions to bring out the idiosyncracies of the subjects, nor permit the investigator to extend the issue in question when necessary. Complete lack of standardization, however, would lead to chaotic results. Hence, the aims of the interview were categorized under seven headings and a number of possible wordings of each question were prepared. Leading questions were avoided, but the precise form of the question was modified wherever necessary to elicit an answer. The atmosphere of the interview was as informal as possible. Rapport and sincerity were achieved in the following ways: 1. The individuals were selected by recommendation and were therefore willing to cooperate. They were not, however, intimates of the experimenter and hence fewer personal barriers of shame or self-consciousness were imposed. 2. The interview was prefaced by the experimenter's statement to the effect that the data were confidential, and that, though they would be published in an academic article, no name would be attached.

The seven aims and categories of questions in the interview were as follows:

1. *Thoughts about Status*

Subject was asked whether he had ever thought *his* standing was *higher* or *lower* than that of other individuals. Where the subject said *yes*, the examiner attempted to find out the frequency of such thoughts. Wherever the subject said *no*, he was asked why he did not think of his status. The reasons for lack of thought were determined for all such subjects wherever possible. While it might be assumed that all individuals in a competitive society would be concerned with status, our own society is not competitive in all respects and the reaction of different individuals to competitive situations is not uniform. Hence, it was necessary to discover empirically whether the subjects were actually concerned with their statuses.

2. *Dimensions of Status*

The subject was asked in what ways he had thought of his status. Here, the attempt was made to elicit all the dimensions of status that he habitually used or thought about. When the subject had ostensibly exhausted the dimensions, the investigator named others to find out their presence or absence.

3. *Frames of Reference*

a. Reference Groups

For each status reported, the subject was asked what group of people he compared himself with. Were they actual people he knew? Were they conceptual or "reified" people whom he did not know, but whose existence he postulated. Were they of higher or lower status than he?

b. Reference Individuals

He was asked for each status whether he compared himself, not with a group, but with a particular, crucial individual, and these individuals were identified.

4. *Genesis of Status*

For each dimension of status reported, he was asked when he had first thought about it (*e.g.*, at what age, at what school level, etc.), the precipitating factors, changes with time in the nature of thoughts about the dimension, affective accompaniments associated with his status, and behavioral consequences of and adjustment to his particular status.

5. *Criteria for the Definition of Status*

For each dimension of status, the subject was asked *how* he decided what his standing was in terms of criteria used.

6. *Values of Different Statuses*

The subject was asked to place the statuses reported in a rank order of values. The question was generally phrased thus: In which standing would you like to be most superior, next most superior, etc., or which status means the most to you, next, etc.

7. *Satisfaction with Status*

The subject was asked which status he was satisfied with, which ones he would like to improve, which he was dissatisfied with, and whether striving for status had been important as a source of motivation to him. He was also asked to judge what would be the maximum and minimum yearly incomes that he would like to have in order to be contended.

Additional facts spontaneously reported and other data that appeared of interest were recorded. Personal data were secured about the individual's name, occupation, education, yearly income, source of income, marital status, parent's status and income, number of siblings, dependents, age, and religion.

Results and Discussion of Results

The results will be treated question by question. Certain of the data are amenable to "quantitative" formulation in terms of fre-

TABLE 2
The Personal Characteristics of the Subjects in the Interview Study

Subject	Sex	Marital Status	Income	Education	Occupation	Religion
1	F	Widow	$2400	Ph.D.	Col. teacher	C*
2	M	Single	600	M.D.	Doctor	J†
3	M	Single	2600	Ph.D.	Col. teacher	J
4	M	Single	1440	M.A.	Fed. clerk	J
5	M	Single	1000	Ph.D.	Student	C
6	M	Married	2400	Ph.D.	Anthropologist	J
7	M	Married	2000	M.D.	Med. student	J
8	M	Married	2500	B.S.	Salesman	J
9	M	Married	1000	A.B.	Student-clerk	J
10	M	Single	600	M.D.	Doctor	J
11	F	Married	2300	M.A.	Bookkeeper	J
12	F	Married	3700	A.B.	Secretary	C
13	F	Married	800	A.B.	Factory clerk	J
14	F	Single	1620	A.B.	Supervis. nurse	C
15	F	Single	1320	In Coll.	Supervis. nurse	C
16	M	Married	4900	A.B.	Editor	J
17	F	Married	4900	A.B.	Housewife	C
18	F	Married	6100	A.M.	Research assoc.	C
19	F	Single	1500	Bus. sch.	Secretary	C
20	F	Widow	336	None	Domestic worker	C
21	F	Single	900	H.S.	Hat check girl	J
22	F	Single	1100	Bus. sch.	Bookkeeper	J
23	M	Married	3000	Ele. sch.	Clerk-retail mgr.	J
24	F	Single	600	Ele. sch.	Waitress	C
25	F	Single	900	Bus. sch.	Stenographer	C
26	F	Married	2912	Bus. sch.	Clerk	J
27	F	Single	1000	2-yr. coll.	Secretary	J
28	F	Single	1100	Bus. sch.	Credit manager	J
29	M	Married	4000	1½-yr. coll.	Consult. chem. eng.	C
30	F	Single	1000	H.S.	Dr.'s receptionist	J
31	M	Single	1100	H.S.	Asst. buyer	J

* Christian.
† Jewish.

quency of given occurrences. Other data will be treated qualitatively. The personal characteristics of all the subjects mentioned below are reported in Table 2.

THOUGHTS OF STATUS

While most of the subjects reported thinking about status, a number of them (6 out of 31) reported practically no thoughts. These data must be considered with two qualifications: 1. Lack of thoughts about status should be regarded probably as lack of concern with status rather than complete absence of the concept of status. 2. Lack of thought may represent verbalized opposition to the concept of status rather than actual absence of its use. Case #3 reports no use of the concept since he regards status as part of a social order that he does not accept. He is annoyed with people who do use a given status as the means to demonstrate their superiority. (This may represent verbalized opposition to the concept rather than actual absence of its use.) Case #6 remarked that he never really *thought* about his status, since he takes for granted his own superiority over other individuals. By implication, this subject *uses* the concept of status but devotes no thoughts to it. Related to #6 is Case #1 who does not consider any traditional status dimensions now. She judges people in terms of what they contribute to social change. Along with this attitude goes a complete lack of ambition to enhance her own status. The basis for lack of ambition lies in the fact that as a child she was taught that there was no status higher than her father's. She has already arrived, and hence there is no higher achievable status.

Subject #27 presents an unusual case. She devotes some thought to status, but her status makes little difference. Thoughts of status are dwarfed by her personal plight and present-day social problems. (She is a German refugee.) She regards difference in status between people as much less important than the *common* social problems of people. Case #30 presents a confused picture. She thinks about matters of status continually but resented E's questions on the subject. She became so emotional during the interview, that an intermission was necessary. She kept saying "that's a rotten word" (status). She says also that she does not go about making obvious status comparisons. There are several reasons for her point of view: 1. She says that she might feel terribly inferior if she made status comparisons. Hence the lack of comparison is partly a protection against insecurity. 2. She has a "radical" point of view; her feeling that status differences may be a function of social dislocation rather than personal lacks. (She is not, however, a member of any radical social movement.) 3. She also has an affective opposition to the concept. E asked why she resented the concept and her answer was, "love of people." She said we had no right to pass judgment on others. It would seem that for her, status differences would place barriers in the way of love of others. Case #31, a member of the Communist Party, thinks of his status in a vicarious way. He thinks of it in terms of elevating the status of others in society, and thus vicariously raising his own. There is very little comparative phrasing of status in terms of *higher* and *lower* position. He reported that even where his status was high he never felt that he was better than any other person. The interpretation of this is partly due to S's conceptualization of the differences, not in terms of personal adequacy but as socially allocated differences. Related to such a view is Case #11 who considers differences in status but does not use them to flaunt her superiority. She understands that superior opportunity has made her superior rather than personal ability. She also values cooperation with others more highly than the enhancement of status differences between people.

It might be thought that all individuals in a competitive society, particularly those drawn from an urban competitive center such as New York, would think of and be striving for high status. Actually, people do not think of status in an indiscriminate fashion. For a variety of reasons, some people, as noted in the above cases, do not use any dimension of status. In two cases the lack of thought correlates with radical attitudes, but this is not characteristic of the four other subjects. As will be shown later, those who do strive for status are selective in using particular statuses rather than all possible statuses. Similarly, there is wide divergence in the amount of concern with status, answers varying from little or no thought to much or continuous thought.

Dimensions of Status

All the dimensions of status reported and their relative frequencies are listed below in Table 3. The meaning of these dimensions of status will be discussed under the treatment of the Criteria by which they are judged.

Reference Groups

The reference groups used are reported in Table 4 for each status with the relative frequencies of occurrence. Some individ-

TABLE 3

THE FREQUENCY OF REPORT FOR VARIOUS DIMENSIONS OF STATUS

Dimension	Frequency	
General	12	
Economic	28	
Intellectual	27	
Social	20	
Looks	18	
Cultural	15	
Athletic	13	(Maximum frequency—31) †
Prestige	12	
Character	4	
Political	2	
Sexual	2	
Religious*	1	
Esteem*	1	

* These dimensions were reported, although the writer questions whether they were really used as statuses.
† Since 31 subjects were used, the maximum possible frequency for a dimension is 31.

uals used several reference groups. For example, a subject might think about his economic status in relation to his friends and the total population. The frequency of such cases is reported in the table under "Frequency of Multiple Reference Groups."

The responses to the question of the reference groups used may be classified under a number of tendencies. Examples of these tendencies are given below.

Variants in Structuring

A few individuals had singularly well structured reference groups which were common to the judgment of all statuses. This was the case with #28 and #21 who use their friends for the judgment of all statuses and #15, a nurse, who uses her occupational group. Hierarchical structuring *within* the reference group as a function of values is illustrated in #6, whose main dimension of status is intellectual. His spontaneously selected reference group is made up of those individuals who write the books he reads. The group is fairly large and amorphous; so the more salient group within it consists of those authors in the sciences and arts which he values most: mathematics, linguistics, anthropology, poetry, and philosophy. Similarly, #9 uses all academic people in the United States as a reference group for intellectual status. (S's aspiration is to do academic work.) This group is large and vague, and the more structured sub-group consists of social scientists. The subject

TABLE 4
The Habitual Reference Groups within Which Status Was Judged

Status	Reference Groups		Frequency of Multiple Reference Groups
Social	Friends	6	
	Work group	4	
	Those in same field	2	
	Similar background	4	
	Neighbors	2	5
	Same race	1	
	Family	1	
	People casually encountered	4	
	Economic classes	2	
Intellectual	Total population	4	
	Acquaintances	12	
	Similar background	4	
	Same occupation	4	
	Work group	4	
	People in contact with in business	1	11
	Same race	1	
	Writers S reads	1	
	People casually encountered	5	
	Definite classes	1	
Cultural	Acquaintances	2	
	Work group	2	
	Same occupation	6	
	Same race	1	
	Great artists	1	2
	People casually encountered	1	
	No reference group*	1	
	No group offered†	2	
Looks	Friends	6	
	Same occupation	2	
	Work group	2	
	Movie actresses	4	7
	People casually encountered	8	
	No reference group	1	
	No group offered	2	
General	Total population	1	
	Same occupation	1	
	People casually encountered	1	0
	No reference group	6	
	No group offered	2	
Economic	Total population	4	
	Friends	10	
	Work group	2	
	Same occupation	5	
	Similar background	1	8
	Employer	2	
	Family	2	
	People casually encountered	10	
	Classes	4	
	No reference group	1	

TABLE 4—(Continued)

Status	Reference Groups		Frequency of Multiple Reference Groups
Prestige	Friends or acquaintances	3	
	Work group	2	
	Definite classes	1	
	Those of very high prestige ("best in field")	2	1
	People casually encountered	3	
	No reference group	1	
	No group offered	1	

* No reference group means that the subject *said* he had no reference group.
† No group offered means that the subject did not volunteer a response or the examiner did not elicit one.

reports that he has no desire to teach other subjects than the social sciences. A variant of hierarchical structuring is the case of #4 whose union was his major reference group. S was one of the leaders in the policy making nucleus within the group. He states that there was no need for comparison with union members below the nucleus. This is due to the fact that the group was organized so that the relations of leaders to ordinary members were formalized.

Class Concepts

A few individuals have elaborate reference groups schematized in class terms. Such is the case with #7 who, for example, states that in the case of social status there are four classes, the ultra, above average, average, and low classes. He compares himself primarily with the above average class of which he is a member, but this class is not nationally represented, *i.e.*, he considers only the above average class in his community. Similarly, #31, a member of the Communist party, has two such reference groups for the judgment of intellectual status. These are respectively: 1. Proletarian intellectuals whom S considers as having higher intellectual status than he has because they have greater knowledge and are putting their knowledge to use. This group is composed of actual friends and acquaintances. 2. Bourgeois Intellectuals, some of whom are former acquaintances and some are conceptual.[1] The members of this group are lower than S in intellectual status, since they are not putting their knowledge to productive use. Similarly, #23, a radical, states that there are three classes in society, the working,

---
[1] S does not know these people. He postulates their existence.

middle, and upper classes. These groups are not face-to-face groups, but portions of the total population. The subject regards himself as between the middle and working classes but identifies himself with the workers. His major reference group consists of the better paid members of the working class. Occasionally, he may compare himself with the middle class because of the fact that he can afford many things which they can. For intellectual status, he uses members of the middle class but only those individuals who are "educated" in the sense of having political sophistication. Class structuring of the reference group is also seen in #17, who uses the total society as a reference group for economic status. She thinks of herself, however, as a white-collar worker and then places this class in the total structure to facilitate a determination of status.

Motivational Processes, Autistic and Realistic, in the Use of the Reference Group

There are certain instances where the use of particular reference groups is autistic, *i.e.*, directed by the subject's motives or desires, where the contradiction with reality is ignored. In other instances the use of the reference group is drive determined but does not stand in major contradiction with reality; the term "realistically motivated" is used in this context.

A case in point is #30, who realistically compares herself with groups who have what she desires. Her reference group for economic status consists of friends who live alone. S states that she is envious of such people. For the same dimension of status she compares herself with friends who have careers. S states that she desires a career. The same individual shows an autistic process in her choice of reference groups for social and intellectual status. In both instances she has two reference groups, one higher in the given status and the other lower. When she uses the higher groups, she says she does not feel that she is lower than they are or inferior to them. With the use of the lower reference groups S states that she feels she is superior in that status. The feeling of superiority exists despite her realization that she should not feel that way, since their lower status may be a function of social dislocation (see case 30 under "thoughts of status"). She rationalizes the mechanics of the upper reference group by saying that she does not feel inferior, since there is always something she can learn to equal them.

Another instance of autism is #29, who reports a reference group for social status the members of which include people like

Sinclair Lewis and Heywood Broun. S would have liked to be in the company of such people, who represent his ideal—intellectually honest, free, and yet funny. For prestige status this same individual uses a reference group composed only of those individuals (men) who are the best in his occupation. The use of the reference groups is unrealistic since the subject can have no actual contact with them. The economic reference group is also representative of his economic aspirations. The group includes a few people who make a little more money than he, and S would like to be able to spend as much as they. He reports less irritation when he thinks of a wealthy reference group than when he thinks of the people who make just a little more money than he.

The case of #27 is an instance of the development of a reference group and the formation of a dimension of status as a result of "realistically motivated" considerations. This German refugee went to a school in Germany along with Nazi pupils. The Nazi children were privileged, but due to mistreatment, the Jewish children began to think that they could not do anything. Jews were not supposed to be good in athletics. S tried to do better in athletics just to show that she could do it. She compared herself with a reference group of Nazi girls, although in normal times (she says) she abhorred competition. Case #15 illustrates temporary changes in the reference group for motivational purposes. For economic status her customary reference group is made up of members of her occupation of her income level. She does, however, compare herself with people of higher and lower incomes when figuring expenditures and says—"if only I were rich" or thinks the converse to the effect that she makes more money than those of lower status and should be able to get along well. Case #24 chooses an autistic reference group when considering her character. She compares herself with girls from "home" who "went wayward." S says she had the same chance as they and did not "go wayward." S thereby feels that her character is superior to other girls. The reference group is apparently chosen with this purpose in mind.

Intra-Individual Comparison

One person, #22, has no salient reference group for any dimension of status. She may use the casual reference group with whom she is in contact at the moment. S phrases her "status" in comparison with herself. She has her own idea of where she should be and asks herself if she is doing as well as she can. Satisfaction with status is a function of such comparison.

Absolute Judgments of Status

Case #19 in considering her athletic status makes the absolute judgment, "lousy." She reports no comparative judgments and states parenthetically that she is always determined to do something about it but never does.

Intra-Individual Judgments and Absolute Judgments imply the absence of an actual reference group and consequently, approximate to the following examples where there is *vocal* rejection of the reference group. Such cases probably represent rejection of status because status by definition demands a reference group for comparison.

Rejection of the Reference Group

One case, #3, rejects the concept of reference group although he does not reject reference individuals. To classify people as members of a given reference group cuts across the situation they are in. He does not look at another person without analyzing his total life situation. The approach is a functional one. An indication of rejection of a reference group for different reasons is seen in Case #4, who was a member of a W.P.A. work group. There was competition for high status within the group, but among certain individuals questions of superior status were set aside because these people were dependent on each other, trusted each other, and all had equality of status within the group.

Summary

Certain interesting facts may be noted in the findings on reference group. The rare occurrence of the total population as a reference group and the great frequency of more intimate reference groups are characteristic of the process of judging status. Individuals operate for the most part in small groups within the total society, and the total population may have little relevance for them. Far more important are their friends, people they work with. Consequently, objective measures of status will very likely differ from subjective measures if total population is the basis for the determination of objective status. Examples have been cited to indicate such processes in connection with the reference group as structuring of the group, possible rejection of the group which would imply rejection of the concept of status, class structuring, autistic distortions, and absolute judgments and intra-individual comparisons of status in the absence of actual reference groups. Extreme reference groups may act via end anchoring[2] or other principles of judgment to enhance status differences. The operation of a given reference group may be affected by various motivational factors, and an extreme reference group may in the presence of these factors not enhance status differences. This is apparent in certain of the above instances where high status groups operate via identification, rationalization, or compensation by the use of an alternative reference group, so as not to cause depreciation in status.

Crucial Reference Individuals

Seventeen subjects reported the use of particular individuals as bases for status comparisons. Fourteen cases did not report such instances. In the great percentage of these latter cases, however, the subjects do make inter-individual comparisons of a casual sort, although their reference individuals are not crucial ones who are always kept in mind. Certain interesting trends may be noted in the use of reference individuals.

Rejection of Reference Individuals as Bases for Status Comparisons

Case #23 says that there are no special individuals who should be used as measures for one's status. This is based on a sort of egalitarian view that all people are fundamentally alike and that

---

[2] When an individual is asked to make absolute judgments upon a group of stimuli, his judgments give evidence that he has formed a scale. This scale is anchored by the end stimuli, so that when the range of stimuli is changed the position of the scale shifts. The scale may be anchored at one end by a presented stimulus which redefines one end of the scale. Such an end anchor causes an extension of the scale toward the specified end, while the scale remains fixed at its other end by the former anchoring stimulus. Consequently, a judgment made formerly, now occupies a different position on the scale since the scale has been extended by the introduction of the new anchoring agent (33, 66, 80, 81). With reference to the status scale, the reference group is analogous to anchoring by the end stimuli. For example, a person's economic status scale (if income is the criterion) may habitually be anchored by the incomes of a Negro share cropper and Henry Ford at the bottom and top ends respectively. When the reference group is changed, the range of values which anchor the status scale shifts. Consequently, a person's subjective status is a function of the reference group which operates through stimulus anchoring. An extreme reference group or reference individual may act in an analogous fashion to an end-anchor. For example, a person whose top end of the economic scale is anchored by a $100,000 a year man has a given status. When the new end-anchor of Henry Ford is presented, the scale is extended and the subject has a lower status. Here the scale has been extended upwards, and a given stimulus, therefore, falls into a lower category than formerly. Hence as the scale moves up, the judgment moves down. This discussion has dealt with the material in the light of actual stimuli. Reference groups are not really presented stimuli. Volkmann, and Volkmann and Hunt (33, 80), however, have shown that values the individual selects and holds in mind operate in the same manner as presented stimuli to anchor the absolute scale.

therefore there are no particular people to be singled out as reference points. Case #11 has no salient reference individuals because she says she is not interested in people very much. Case #7 states that he does not believe in using particular reference individuals. He knows wealthy friends but he does not go around wishing he were like them. Perhaps the subject rejects an obvious reference individual to avoid depreciation in his status.

Reference Individuals as Aspiration Levels

In talking of the genesis of intellectual status, Case #5, a psychologist, indicates two reference individuals acting as aspiration points. He says that he began to compare himself with Pavlov and Helmholtz and states that the greatest achievement or status that he could think of would have been to bring back one of Pavlov's dogs from Russia. Here is a graphic instance of the inability to understand the individual's view of his intellectual status without knowledge of this unusual reference point for the judgment of status. Another example of the same trend is Case #12, a secretary, who uses her boss, her boss's boss, and the top boss as well as certain people in the Blue Book for comparisons of prestige. She states that these people have more prestige than she, but that she never thinks of people lower in prestige. She is uncomfortable with these reference individuals. By using such individuals, this subject's judgment of her status should be lowered, but she apparently gets a sort of vicarious prestige from identifying with reference individuals of higher status. Likewise Case #29 compares his intellectual status with Steinmetz and Berzelius. He always compares himself unfavorably with these individuals. Yet he probably uses them as aspiration points. Case #6 uses as reference individuals the people for whom he has most admiration, such as Ruth Benedict and Franz Boas, who represent admired persons in his own profession. Another example is Case #24 who compares her intellectual and cultural status with her aunt, and says if she were like her aunt she'd be a perfect woman. She also uses an aspiration individual for character judgments, her mother, whom she has never known and who died when she was an infant. Case #13 illustrates a reference individual involving autistic processes. A particular woman whom this subject knows is the reference individual for all statuses. This person is particularly attractive and superior in all status respects. The dimension in which she particularly compares herself is pulchritude, which represents the only dimension in which she can possibly compete with this person.

Reference Individuals Chosen by Virtue of Affinity or Contrast with the Subject

The reference individuals in many cases are chosen by virtue of similarity to the subject, proximity to him in life situation, or as the result of objective facts which facilitate such comparison. The term *affinity* is used to cover such instances. Other reference individuals are chosen for comparisons of status by virtue of contrast with the subject's status. They are so different from him that they stand out as sources for comparison. The following cases illustrate these processes. An example is Case #15 who uses a good friend for comparison in social status. This reference individual does not get along as well with others as she herself does. In trying to find out the basis for this and to help her she has become conscious of comparisons of status. Case #28 illustrates a similar process. She used to compare her social status with a girl who went out socially quite often, whereas she did not. The subject felt unhappy and felt that there was something wrong with her. The comparisons continued because she knew the girl well. Whenever this subject saw her or called her on the telephone, she found out that she had a date. Thus objective proximity and contact facilitated the comparison.

Cases in which familiarity or similarity between the reference individual and the subject is operative are illustrated by #20 whose reference individual for all status dimensions is a person who belongs to the same church and whom she has known since they were children. They played together and today have about the same status. Case #21 possibly illustrates this process as well as a degree of autism. Her reference individual for attractiveness is Rita Hayworth since many friends have said that the two look alike.

Instances of "contrast" are seen in cases in which certain individuals are reference points because they contrast with the subject or because they stand out and are easy to use as reference individuals. Subject #9 reports that for cultural status the manager of the bookstore where he works acts as a reference individual. The man is very different from the subject. The manager is particularly distinctive in his own shop, since he has no knowledge of literature and the arts. This subject also states that Robert Lynd is a reference individual for intellectual status because he is so different from other academic people. Other examples reported are: strikingly beautiful or ugly women, people of great superiority, people of great personal attraction, brilliant classmates, disliked or admired people, very thrifty or extravagant people.

Autistic Tendencies in the Use of Reference Individuals

Case #27 uses her mother as a reference individual in considering character and intellectual status. S feels that she is of higher character and intellectual status than her mother, and consequently feels superior through the comparison. Case #28 uses one female friend as a reference individual for the judgment of economic status. S is much better off than her friend and feels *happy* by comparison. Yet she does not feel *superior* as a result of the comparison and there is little emotional involvement. The reason lies in the general finding reported before. Where the status of another person or the subject can be removed from personal focus and interpreted as someone else's fault or the fault of the social order, there is little inferiority feeling, as in this case. S states that her friend's low economic status is a consequence of dependency upon her parents. Consequently, it is not her friend's fault. The case suggests that such "social displacement" may not represent a rationalization to enhance the subject's status, since in this case it operates to rob the subject of any enhancement of status.

Imposition of the Dimension by the Reference Individual

In the preceding cases the subjects have had a dimension of status and have then considered certain reference groups in judging status within that dimension. In the following instances the presence of a given reference group operates to impose a dimension of status not formerly present. By way of analogy, when a person goes to a baseball game and sees the players he may start thinking about athletic status or his own standing in relation to the players, or a person invited to J. P. Morgan's home may begin thinking about his relative financial standing. This process is somewhat akin to a set imposed by the presence of another person which then specifies the aspect perceived or judged. Such processes are noted in the following: Case #3 reports that he never spontaneously considers income or economic status, but when he sees people who are earning much more or much less than their deserts he begins to think about economic status. S regards such people as representatives of a dislocated social order. They arouse annoyance and contempt in S if they try to appear superior by means of high incomes. Likewise, Case #18 states that she rarely thinks of economic status spontaneously. If she is confronted by some situation in which there is a person of much lower economic status, S thinks of the dimension and feels sorry for these people. She says that she feels no ego-enhancement in such situations. Similarly, if she is confronted by people exceedingly high in economic status, the dimension becomes salient. In such instances, however, the subject states that she is not personally involved. She may either feel amused and say to herself that she is happier than they or feel resentment toward the situation when she realizes that others are impoverished.

First Recollections of Status

In Table 5, a frequency distribution is presented indicating the age at which various subjects first recollected that they became concerned with particular statuses. In the following discussion "genesis" of status refers to the recollection of the earliest concern with status. The results are of limited significance for the following reasons: 1. Only a limited number of subjects were able to state the approximate age for the appearance of given statuses. Most often the subject woud say that he had thought of economic status, for example, when he was in public school or high school. Errors in the ability to recollect first thoughts of status are probably large. 2. Age has different meaning for different statuses. For certain statuses age is not significant since such dimensions may be precipitated by a variety of experiences. The age of genesis varies with the incidence of these experiences. For example, the incidence of economic status varies from six to twenty. Early genesis was associated with such factors as death of parents, necessity of working, and privation at an early age. Later genesis in adolescence was often associated with the need of money so as to be successful socially. Late genesis in adult life may be associated with the end of school, the independence of the subject, and the necessity of work. For other status dimensions age is significant.. Thoughts of these dimensions may be limited or emphasized by certain stages of development. For example, the genesis of athletic status occurs from the ages of five to ten. Such genesis is probably associated with the common childhood value of physical achievement and the great role of play activities.

A number of hypotheses may be offered concerning the genesis of status.

1. Status dimensions are precipitated by given kinds of experiences or limited or emphasized by given stages of development.

2. Different status dimensions develop at different times, and concern with status is historically specific. No subject reported a general notion of status out of which particular statuses individu-

TABLE 5
Distribution of Ages at Which Subjects First Became Concerned with Various Statuses

Age	Economic	Intellectual	Cultural	Social	Looks	Prestige	Athletic
4	......	1	......	......	1	......	......
5	......	......	......	......	1	......	1
6	1	1	......	......	1	......	3
7	1	4	1	......	......	......	......
8	1	1	......	2	......	......	1
9	1	1	......	......	......	......	1
10	1	......	......	1	3	1	1
11	......	1	......	......	......	......	......
12	1	2	2	1	1	1	......
13	1	......	......	......	......	1	......
14	2	......	......	1	3	......	......
15	2	2	1	......	2	......	......
16	2	1	......	3	......	......	......
17	4	1	2	......	......	1	......
18	1	1	3	2	......	......	......
19	1	......	......	1	1	......	......
20	1	......	......	......	......	......	......
31	......	......	......	......	......	1	......
N	20	16	9	11	13	5	7

ated. The tendency towards specificity is supported by the different ages at which particular statuses appear, and the different experiences which give rise to specific dimensions. Also, relatively few subjects reported a general status at all. Another factor will be made clear in Chapter V on General Status. Differences in status between different dimensions of status are relatively large, *e.g.*, a person may have an economic status of 70 and an intellectual status of 30. If there were some common level of general status, there would be more similarity in the judgments of specific statuses. However, status dimensions are related functionally and one can serve to compensate for another, or one status may be precipitated by another status which the subject regards as inadequate.

3. Statuses operate with other variables to determine feelings of security. Low status may act as a potent source of insecurity feelings, and high status may serve various ego needs. When a given status no longer serves a function in the personality it may lose importance or vanish. Such dynamic tendencies may be offset by a number of factors. For example: a. Low status may not correspond with inferiority feelings if the subject interprets such status as a consequence of social dislocation rather than personal inadequacy. b. Low status may not serve to produce inferiority if the reference group has the same status and there is consequently

little opportunity for invidious comparison. c. Low status may not be associated with much affect if the dimension of experience is not valued by the subject.

4. Striving for high status is directed in specific channels. One protocol, Case #3, will be presented to indicate many of these trends. His first experiences of intellectual status were in elementary school when he found out that he was a superior student. Yet he says that he did not get much pleasure from superior status for several reasons. 1. He did not like being thought superior since it meant being exposed to public scrutiny. Such exposure was painful to him and his extreme bashfulness outweighed any of the advantages of superior status. 2. He felt that this achievement was what he was competent to do and some pleasure was derived from having done a good job. (There is considerable ambivalence in this instance between the pleasure of achievement and the painful feeling of public exposure.) 3. He did not care much about intellectual status because he had the other children's values which emphasized athletic ability. Consequently, when he became a good athlete at about the age of twelve, he derived great pleasure. Athletic status became most important and he was apologetic about being a good student. His high status served the function of making him feel a more well-rounded person, whereas previously he had felt one-sided because of the attitude of his playmates towards him as an intellectual. The athletic dimension became less important with age. However, it is still present to some degree and he derives enjoyment from being a good ball player. It did lose potency because he developed security by other means and it was no longer needed.

Thoughts of economic status were precipitated by early experiences of being poor. His parents were in dire economic straits and, even at the pre-school level, low status was a potent factor in his insecurity. His extreme bashfulness and sensitiveness reinforced by social stigmatization made him feel worse. This economic area of insecurity narrowed because he noted that all the other people he knew were in the same economic position. He also says that with maturity and a body of knowledge within which to interpret his status, feelings of insecurity lessened. He realized that low economic status was not his fault but due to social dislocation. He put his childhood experience into this context, and this social perspective tended to throw thoughts of his economic status out of awareness and continually reinforced the dissociation of economic factors and feelings of security.

Status as a Means to an End

Other examples of the "rise and fall" of a dimension of status in accordance with its functional value to the individual are seen in several women subjects. These data were reported only by women and reflect probably a sex difference in respect of the degree to which the status dimension of looks is emphasized in our culture for women rather than men. Subjects #12, #13, and #20 thought about the matter of their looks a good deal until they were married, at which time the dimension ceased to be important. Looks were conceived of as a means through which they might get married and once marriage was achieved the subjects no longer needed high status in respect of looks. In addition, marriage demonstrated the adequacy of their looks, hence worry about the dimension ceased. An analogous instance is Case #11 who says that at 18, she would have much preferred being told she was beautiful to being told she had a mind. Today, looks are unimportant to her. She says "My husband thinks I'm beautiful." Other instances in which looks were demonstrated by success with men are Cases #18, #24, and #17. Number seventeen says that at the age of 16 she thought she was the "world's ugliest duckling," but when she achieved social success with a beau, her estimation of her looks went up. Similar data of interest are found in Case #21 where there was no need for the dimension in her doings with men. She says that she did not worry about looks since the dates with the men she knew were not on the basis of looks. Then at the age of 19 she became concerned with looks since she conceived of looks as an instrumentality in dramatic success which is her goal.

Not all women used looks as such an instrumentality. Case #26 reports that she was always conscious of her looks and that after marriage, looks became even more important to her. Looks are not regarded as a device to get men since she says she wanted to be attractive even with girls. She likes to look well at all times, and looks imply rather an aesthetic dimension for her. Consequently, there was no change after marriage.

Examples of other statuses used as instrumentalities may be seen in Case #29 who is concerned with his prestige, which is a very important factor in his capacity as a consulting chemist. Case #18 indicates the loss of a status dimension when it no longer served a purpose. This subject was very conscious of her high social standing when she reached high school. When she found out she was not wanted within the group, she realized that people must like you for other reasons more important than social status. Then she was accepted in the group because of her abilities rather than her social status. These facts operated to vitiate the importance of this status.

Instances of Changes in Status for Motivational Reasons

Case #10, an Italian Refugee, said cultural status first assumed importance for him when he came to America. In Italy, culture had been important, but not as a tool with which to manifest superior status. There was little need to enhance his status while in Italy. In America, with the feeling of continual need to enhance his status, his cultural knowledge became used in a competitive way as an instrument of high status. Number five sought high intellectual status and his main intellectual aspirations up to this period were in the arts. He began to discover his inadequacy in this field, and was afraid to compete. Yet he wanted to assert his superiority. He sought another avenue for high intellectual status and choose a field in which he thought there were few people, *i.e.*, Psychology (and now he wonders). Here is an instance of changing a status dimension when it does not function adequately. Similarly #9 placed tremendous emphasis on intellectual status. He sought a way to assert his superiority, and high status in a number of dimensions was precluded for various reasons. Consequently, he found intellectual status the only dimension in which to assert his desire for high status.

Development of Dimension by Specific Experience

A graphic instance of the development of thoughts of low status and their decline or vitiation is Case #27 who at the age of 12–13 studied "The Science of Races" in a German school. Movies of beautiful Nordic girls were shown and contrasted with pictures of ugly Non-Aryans. At first she thought she was not beautiful, that the teaching was correct, and that she looked like the pictures of the Non-Aryans. She felt very unhappy, but later reversed her opinion of her status. Parental and friendly tuition helped to change her mind. The incident that discredited in her mind the Nazi teaching about beauty came when the girls took measurements of cephalic index on each other and she found that she was dolichocephalic.

Two specific factors seem to be conducive to thoughts of intellectual status. Nine subjects (5, 8, 9, 13, 16, 17, 18, 10) reported that they thought of their intellectual status at an early age. In all these instances the two factors present were great family emphasis on academic achievement and attendance at a competitive school where competition was emphasized. Of ten subjects (15, 1, 23, 30, 19, 26, 28, 31, 27, 29) who developed thoughts of intellectual status at a late age, four reported absence of these factors, four had both these factors present in their history, and two had but one factor present. Thus, while these social factors are conducive to development of such thoughts they are not essential.

Striving for Status within Specific Channels

Several instances of striving for status directed in specific channels are presented. Case #22 had a great deal of prestige in her home town. The subject now lives in New York and has much less prestige. However, she does not feel insecure and is not striving for prestige. She rates prestige as the least valued of the six statuses, and also knew that when she came to New York she would have to sacrifice some prestige. Other statuses, however, more valued by the subject might be enhanced. Therefore, this loss means little to her. Subject #4 interprets his own case as follows: At an early age in his history he sought highest status in all respects, in all groups, and on all occasions. He finally realized his own limitations and the impossibility of the above goal. He still wanted high status in general, but he now decided to strive selectively to achieve this. He chose specific dimensions in which he might be successful in given groups and now competes for high status on these terms.

Similarity of Status in the Reference Group

There are two consequences of similarity of status in the reference group. A. Thoughts of status may be associated with little inferiority because of the equality of status of the reference group. For example, Subject #20 stated that she began to work when she was twelve. She began to think about her economic status at this time and felt very bad that she was poor. She did not, however, feel inferior to others because all the people she associated with were equally poor. B. The lack of differences in status in the reference group may prevent the arousal of thoughts of status. This is indicated in the following cases: Subject #27 noted no differences in social status until she went to a party and saw how people in other social strata lived. Up to this time she had operated in one social milieu, and had gone to a private school, where the individuals all came from the same income group. Case #24 said that she had little knowledge of differences in economic status until she was about 19. She had gone to a clerical school and all the girls wore uniforms so that differences in the economic status of the girls mediated via differences in clothing were not noticed.

Changes in Affect with "Displacement" of the Cause

A Negro subject stated that she does not feel bad about her looks because "the Lord made us that way." Consequently, she can't do anything about it to change her status. The converse of this situation may also occur. Case #22 felt bad about her low economic status while she was dependent on her parents, instead of displacing the affect to them. When she began to work she no longer felt bad despite low status, because the power of manipulation of status was now in her own hands.

THE CRITERIA FOR STATUS

Each subject reported the criterion or criteria by which he judged each of the status dimensions he recognized. This is an important variable in subjective status since a person's status varies with the criteria used. Tables are presented below for various statuses of the frequency of occurrence of given criteria in all cases where the status was mentioned. These frequencies add up to a greater number than the number of reports of the given status, since most individuals use multiple criteria for each dimension.

These data are very indicative of possible discrepancies between objective and subjective status, *e.g.*, only 13 people used income *per se* for economic status. Standard of living is the more frequent measure, and two people with the same income may regard themselves as of different economic status if their living conditions are different. Hence, measures of status in accordance with income may be completely different from the person's judgment. Similarly, measures of objective status which use a unitary criterion for the determination of status will depart from it because most people use multiple criteria. This complication is encountered in all dimensions of status, and subjective status can only be determined by knowledge of personal criteria.

SATISFACTION WITH STATUS AND VALUES

Various examples of the importance of values have been presented in different parts of the discussion of the interview material. Striving for status is generally directed in the channel of the valued status. Degree of dissatisfaction with a given status varies inversely with status, providing there is high valuation of the status dimension. Satisfaction with status is consequently, also a function

TABLE 6

The Criteria for the Judgment of Status

Status	Criteria		Frequency of Multiple Criteria*
Social	Background of family	7	
	Membership in special groups	3	
	Breeding	1	
	People S. knows	4	
	Money	2	
	Dates, getting along with those of other sex	3	
	Ability to get along with others	5	5
	Pleasant personality	3	
	Degrees	1	
	Achievements	2	
	Race	2	
	Character	1	
	Intrinsic qualities	1	
	Social esteem	2	
	By other standards	2	
	Not offered†	2	
Intellectual	Formal education	19	
	Understanding, reasoning, ability, intelligence	27	
	Social intelligence	3	
	Broadness of knowledge	13	
	Knowledge and appreciation of arts	6	
	Knowledge put to use	1	
	Amount of reading	3	22
	Amount of worldly experience	10	
	Achievements	3	
	Adaptability	1	
	Academic background of family	1	
	Intellectual curiosity	1	
	Ability to discuss and theoretical approach	3	
	Character	3	
Economic	Income	13	
	Standard of living	26	
	Aspirations and future possibilities	12	22
	Dependents	9	
	Security of income	1	
	Source of income	1	
	Not offered	1	
Cultural	Achievement in and knowledge of arts	11	
	Appreciation of arts	10	
	Wide knowledge, broad interests	4	10
	Manners and behavior in social situations	1	
	Preciousness about art‡	1	
	Not offered	1	

TABLE 6.—(Continued)

Status	Criteria		Frequency of Multiple Criteria*
Looks	"Looks"	5	
	Intelligent look	1	
	Grooming and style	3	
	Facial beauty	1	3
	Personality	1	
	Amount of success with and attention from other sex	2	
	Not offered	10	
General	Education	1	
	Understanding of world	1	
	Intelligence	1	
	Nature of work (creative, etc.)	1	1
	Probably composite of other statuses	1	
	Not offered	8	
Prestige	Social recognition, esteem, reputation	8	
	Social standing	2	
	Influence or power	2	
	Leadership	1	7
	Accomplishments	3	
	Integrity	1	
	Economic standing	1	
	Kind of job	1	

* If a subject, for example, used standard of living, future possibilities, and source of income as criteria for economic status, it was considered a case of multiple criteria. Frequency of multiple criteria represents the number of such cases.

† Subject did not offer or examiner did not elicit the criteria.

‡ The operation of this criterion for this subject is unidirectional. Other criteria may raise or lower a person's status depending on their magnitude. In this instance "preciousness" is always used to lower status.

of the reference group, since the reference group is a variable in the judgment. Furthermore, status is a function of valuation of the reference group, as in the case of #18, who says that her status only concerns her within the context of a reference group of professional associates, and that her status outside of these groups makes no difference to her.

Satisfaction with status is also a function of aspiration for status. Mere position is not indicative of satisfaction. A person of low status may not feel inferior if he has no higher aspiration in that direction. This result may be indicated in the material on economic status. Besides reporting his income, each subject reported his aspirations for income. There were 24 cases for whom data on economic aspiration, income and satisfaction were available. Eighteen were dissatisfied with their economic status, and 6 were satisfied. In the satisfied subjects the income range was from $900–$6100 a year, so that mere income does not specify satisfaction. Similarly, in the dissatisfied cases the income range was from $336–$4000 a year, so that mere income does not specify dissatisfaction with status.[3] Two contrasting cases may illustrate this point. One subject who earns $336 a year from Relief and domestic work says that if she had an income of $900 "I'd be joyous over it" and that with $500 a year, she could live happily. As a contrast, a person who earned $3676 a year, valued economic status first of six statuses, and reported an aspiration of $25,000.

Mean data were secured on these two groups and are presented, though they obscure the individual trend, and although six cases in the satisfied group are not an adequate sample. Aspiration for income was treated in terms of the difference between desired income and actual income expressed as a percent increment of the actual income.

The mean increment for the dissatisfied group was 836.7% and for the satisfied group 290.4.% This means that the dissatisfied people wanted on the average to increase their incomes to about eight times the present level and the satisfied to about three times the present level.[4]

These data may explain Kornhauser's (39) finding of almost as much dissatisfaction in the middle income group as in the low income groups. The explanation of his results may lie in the relation of aspiration to income.

Summary

A series of intensive interviews on a fairly heterogeneous population has indicated a number of independent variables such as the individual's values, reference group, aspiration level, and criteria for judgment which must be taken into account in the understanding of subjective status. Under each of these headings the various modes of response have been stated. Findings on thoughts of status, genesis of status, motivation and status, and the emotional accompaniments of given status have also been reported.

---

[3] While there is a slight difference in the level of income for the two groups, the difference is probably not significant.

[4] The magnitude of these increments is a function of the question which was worded as follows: "What is the *maximum* income that you would like to have in order to be satisfied?" The magnitude of the aspiration would have been less with different wording, but the contrasting result for both groups is probably not an artefact.

CHAPTER III

THE CONSTRUCTION OF A RELIABLE SCALE FOR THE MEASUREMENT OF STATUS

INTRODUCTION

On the basis of the interview material certain independent variables were identified as operative in the field of judgments of status, and several experiments were designed to study the effect of these variables. The first problem, however, was to devise a scale for the measurement of subjective status. In order to note the effect of the independent variables it is necessary to measure the dependent variable, *i.e.*, status, and therefore some scale was needed.

Certain postulates led to the form of the present scale, as well as certain interview findings.

1. Since status refers to position in relation to other people, the scale should be phrased in terms of people.

2. Since the judgments are made in relation to different reference groups of individuals, the scale should specify not people in general, but particular reference groups.

3. The scale could not be phrased in terms of absolute numbers of people since different reference groups differ in absolute size, and a common scale was needed to serve for all the reference groups used. Consequently, the scale should refer to given proportions of any reference group specified.

4. A given dimension of status may be judged in terms of different criteria and a person's status is a function of the criteria used. Therefore, the criteria of the scale must be specified. This is true since all subjects should be judging a dimension of status with the same criteria and without explicit statement there would be no assurance that such was the case.

5. It was felt that the scale should allow the subject to judge other people as being of the same status. Some degree of false precision, not characteristic of the usual situation, would be imposed on the judgments if the subject had no way of indicating uncertainty or sameness of status for the reference group.

Two graphic rating scales were used for each judgment. The reference group within which the subject judged his status was specified on each of the scales and the scales were divided off into percents of the specified reference group. The status to be judged on the scale was designated, and the definition of the dimension phrased in terms of a set of criteria was written on the bottom of the sheet. One scale referred to those lower than the subject in the given status, and the other scale to those higher. A sample scale is presented in Figure 1 with the total population as the reference group.

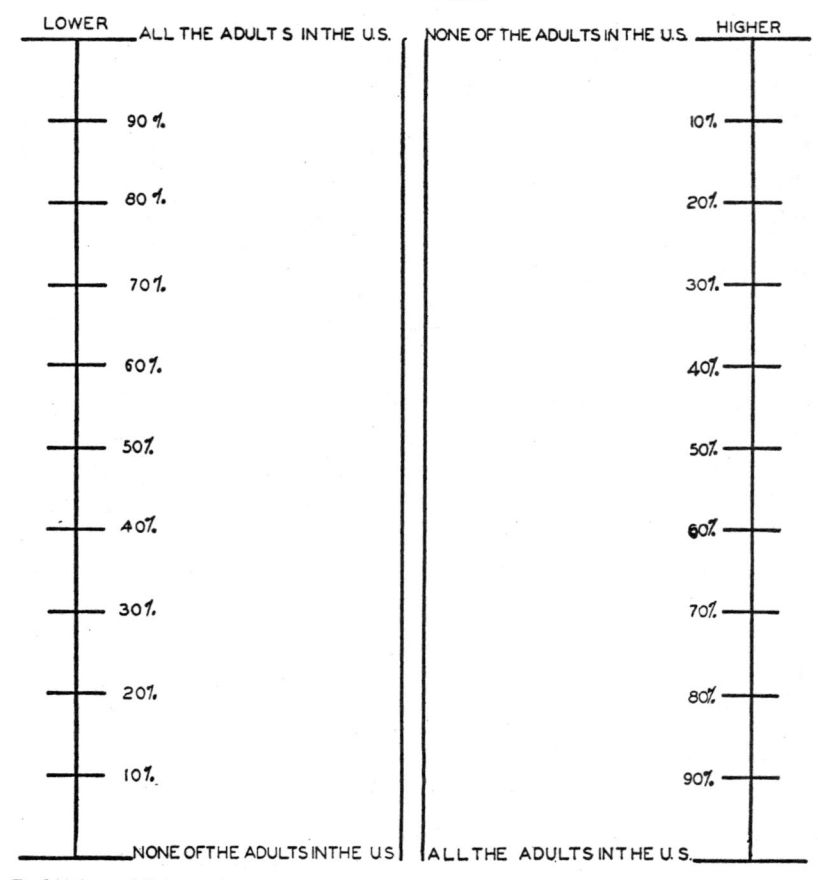

Status Dimension

```
LOWER   ALL THE ADULTS IN THE U.S.    NONE OF THE ADULTS IN THE U.S.   HIGHER

           90%                                          10%

           80%                                          20%

           70%                                          30%

           60%                                          40%

           50%                                          50%

           40%                                          60%

           30%                                          70%

           20%                                          80%

           10%                                          90%

        NONE OF THE ADULTS IN THE U.S.   ALL THE ADULTS IN THE U.S.
```

Definition of Dimension

FIG. 1. The sample status scale.

The following instructions were given orally with the aid of a chart which was a replica of the scales the subjects had. The instructions covered the following points but were not read. In order to preserve spontaneity, the wording, as well, was not precisely adhered to in all instances.

This is an experiment on people's views of their own position in society. You may not know the actual answers to some of these questions, but we are interested in your *opinions* about your own standing. In this experiment you make certain judgments about certain of your standings.

(The subjects were then told to open their booklets to the first page where a sample scale was presented, *i.e.*, athletic standing in relation to all the adults in N.Y.C. The examiner then explained the instructions with the aid of his chart.)

Now supposing we were interested in what you thought your athletic standing was in relation to all the adults in N.Y.C. The two lines on the page stand for all the adults in N.Y.C. This point (the examiner designated a point on the scale) indicates all the adults, this point none of the adults, this point 10%, etc. Now supposing you thought about 50% of all the adults in N.Y.C. were lower than you in athletic ability you would make a mark on the line marked lower next to 50%. You may make the mark anywhere along the line—it does not have to be next to the numbers. (Here the examiner gave further examples of judgments.) Now supposing you had made this mark and I now asked you what percent of the adults in N.Y.C. you were *fairly certain* are lower than you in athletic standing, you might change your former mark because you might be uncertain about some of the people.

The line marked higher also stands for all the adults in N.Y.C. but this time the direction of the numbers is reversed. Now, supposing you had said 50% of the adults were lower than you and I asked you what percent of the adults in N.Y.C. you were fairly certain are higher than you in athletic standing. You might not necessarily say 50% because you might think that some people have the same standing as you.

The two marks cannot possibly add up to more than 100% since there are only 100% of people, but they do not have to add up to as much as 100%.

The examiner then answered all questions before proceeding to the actual judgments. The instructions were given in the same fashion for all the following scales.

Now turn the page. This time you will note you have to judge your . . . standing which is defined for you at the bottom of the page, and this time the lines refer to . . . (reference group). So you make a mark on the line marked lower indicating what percent of the . . . (reference group) you are fairly certain are lower than you in . . . standing and a mark on the line marked higher indicating what percent you are fairly certain are higher than you.

In this fashion the instructions and scale specified the reference group, a judgment at points other than the indicated deciles, the criteria and the dimension to be judged, a given certainty criterion, and a "three category" judgment allowing for uncertainty or identity of status.

There was a relatively large number of statuses which might be worked with, as well as a large number of reference groups. Each status, as well, was not a unitary discriminable aspect and there were multiple criteria by which it could be defined. For practical purposes only certain statuses, reference groups, and discriminable aspects were used.

The interview material was an empirical justification for the choices made. The five most frequently mentioned specific statuses were chosen, in addition to general status, which was selected as one dimension worthy of experimental study. Three reference groups were used and these were chosen because they occurred frequently in the interview material, and because they were contrasted in size, composition, or nature.

The dimensions were: General, Economic, Intellectual, Cultural, and Social status, and Physical attractiveness.

The reference groups were: Total adult population in the United States, friends and acquaintances, and the occupational group.

For the specification of the criteria and the discriminable aspects we again found the interview material helpful. 1. It was decided to define each dimension not as a single discriminable aspect and to use multiple criteria. This was due to the fact that subjects in the interview study reported that they used multiple criteria to judge each dimension of status. Hence, some sacrifice in the unitariness of the aspect was made for the sake of maintaining the common situation of judgment. 2. The multiple criteria were chosen on the basis of their frequency of occurrence in the interview data, providing these criteria were not antithetical in nature.

The definitions of the dimensions follow:

Intellectual Standing refers to the amount and kind of education you have had, your general knowledge, and your ability to reason and understand things.

Economic Standing refers to your actual income, taking into account also the number of persons dependent on you, the way you live, and your prospects for advancement.

Cultural Standing refers to how much you know about and whether you appreciate such things as music, painting, and literature.

Social Standing refers to the kind of family you come from, the kind of breeding you have, and the kind of people you know.

Physical Attractiveness is self-explanatory and should be judged only in relation to others of your own sex.

Total Standing refers to your general position in relation to others according to whatever standard or combination of standards you think enter into general standing. (General Standing was defined in a tautological fashion for reasons which will be made clear in Chapter V.)

Each subject was given a booklet which included 18 such rating scales (a scale for each of the three reference groups and for each of the six statuses) plus the sample scale for athletic standing and a personal data sheet for age, sex, etc.

Scoring

The index of a person's status in all cases was the percent of the reference group lower in the given status plus half the middle category (*i.e.*, plus half the percent of the reference group with the same status).

RELIABILITY

Procedure

The reliability of the scales was secured by repeating all the judgments after a two week interval. At the second session the original instructions were repeated and prefaced by the statement:

> The first thing we have to do is take over the test we did last time. In order to find out a certain thing it is necessary to give the material twice. It will not be given a third time. However, we do need it twice. The results this time are just as important as the first results. This does not mean that you did not do well the first time; everybody in the group did well, but all the people in the experiment are doing this twice.

These instructions were neutral so as not to facilitate change or constancy in the judgments, and they were intended to keep motivation as high as possible. Additional information was secured at the end of the second session as to whether any objective change in S's situation had occurred during the interval. This was done by the following question:

> Have any changes in any of your standings since you last filled out this form occurred, such as changes in your economic standing like losing your job, or change in your salary? If so, indicate these changes.

Cases in which such changes had occurred were relatively few and these subjects were not included in the reliability calculations.

Subjects

The subjects numbered 41, 18 women and 23 men; 20 of the individuals were married; 16 had college training; 23 high school training, and 2 had only elementary school training. None of these subjects had been used in the interview study. Frequency-distributions of ages and incomes follow:

TABLE 7
Ages and Incomes of the Subjects in the Reliability Study

Age	Frequency	Income	Frequency
17–20	9	0– 499	2
21–24	12	500– 999	9
25–28	5	1000–1499	7
29–32	2	1500–1999	2
33–36	2	2000–2499	3
37–40	4	2500–2999	4
41–44	5	3000–3499	3
45–48	1	3500–3999	2
Unspecified	1	4000–4499	2
	—	4500–4999	1
	41	5000–5499	2
		8000–plus	1
		Unspecified	3
			—
			41

The occupations included 16 housewives, 6 clerks, 3 in business, 2 engineers, 4 in machine or mechanical work, 1 waiter, 1 chauffeur, 1 seaman, 1 salesgirl, 1 social worker, 1 technician, 1 college assistant, 1 typesetter, 1 wireman. One person did not specify his occupation.

TABLE 8
The Reliability of Subjective Status as a Function of the Reference Group, Dimension of Status, and Sex of the Sample

	General	Economic	Intellectual	Cultural	Social	Attractiveness
	(Combined populations)					
Total population	.74	.45	.75	.78	.52	.50
Friends	(.17)*	.37	.48	.50	.39	.76
Occupation	.58	.57	.54	.76	.49	.50
	(Male population)					
Total population	.72	(.32)	.70	.66	(.40)	.67
Friends	(.33)	(.37)	.48	.62	.48	.82
Occupation	.56	.54	.51	.72	(.25)	.70
	(Female population)					
Total population	.75	.53	.78	.84	.60	(.34)
Friends	(.06)	(.37)	(.48)	(.40)	(.32)	.70
Occupation	.60	.69	.56	.78	.62	(.34)

* Parentheses indicate non-significance.

Results

Reliability coefficients were calculated for the male, female, and combined populations for all statuses and all reference groups. These are presented in Table 8. The significance of the difference from zero was calculated by the transmutation of the r's into Fisher's Z-correlation function.

TABLE 8a

THE SIGNIFICANCE OF THE RELIABILITY COEFFICIENTS AS INDICATED BY THE CRITICAL RATIOS FOR THE DIFFERENCES BETWEEN OBTAINED COEFFICIENTS AND ZERO
T–values, 40 degrees of freedom, 5% level of significance—2.02
20 degrees of freedom, 5% level of significance—2.09
15 degrees of freedom, 5% level of significance—2.13

	General	Economic	Intellectual	Cultural	Social	Attractiveness
	(Combined population, N = 41)					
Total population	5.59	2.85	5.72	6.15	3.39	3.23
Friends	(1.01)*	2.28	3.08	3.23	2.42	5.86
Occupation	3.89	3.81	3.55	5.86	3.15	3.23
	(Male population, N = 23)					
Total population	4.12	(1.51)	3.61	3.60	(1.93)	3.68
Friends	(1.56)	(1.76)	2.38	3.30	2.38	5.26
Occupation	2.63	2.75	2.56	4.13	(1.16)	3.94
	(Female population, N = 18)					
Total population	3.74	2.27	4.02	4.70	2.66	(1.36)
Friends	(.21)	(1.49)	(2.01)	(1.63)	(1.28)	3.34
Occupation	2.66	3.26	2.43	4.02	2.79	(1.26)

* Parentheses indicate critical ratios that do not meet the 5% level of significance.

DISCUSSION OF RESULTS

These reliabilities range from .06–.84, 34 of the 54 coefficients being .50 or over. They compare favorably with the r's reported for other rating scales in the literature. Symonds (77) reports an r of .55 as typical for ratings of personality traits. Kornhauser (40) reports an r of .58 as the highest r in the correlation of the ratings of three judges. Hartshorne and May (29) report a repeat r of .69 and an average r for the ratings of three teachers of .57. Shen (71) reports an average r of .55. The American Council on Education scale (6) yields from .35 to .73 for the ratings of three judges. Consequently, the reliability of our instrument seems sufficiently high to justify its use in further experimental work.

Certain interesting trends are noted in the reliabilities. Of the 13 reliability coefficients that are insignificant, 8 are for the friends reference group. Despite the habitual use of friends as a reference group (as reported in the interview material), individuals are unable to judge reliably within this group. Thus reliability is a function of the reference group. In all such instances where the judgment is unreliable in relation to friends, it is reliable for other reference groups. Therefore it is not the dimension of status that is unreliable, but judgments of the dimension within certain reference groups. (The relation of reliability to the reference group will be discussed further in Chapter IV.)

Sex differences and dimension differences in reliability may also be noted, *e.g.*, the consistent tendency for men to judge attractiveness more reliably than women, the greater inadequacy of the friends reference group for the women subjects. The author is unable to account for these differences at the present stage of investigation.

CHAPTER IV

THE RELATION OF THE REFERENCE GROUP TO JUDGMENTS OF STATUS

INTRODUCTION

Status, by definition, refers to the relative position of individuals, and it is obvious that depending on who the other individuals are, a person's conception of his own position will change. For example, if one considers successively his economic status in relation to Henry Ford and to a sharecropper in the South, he will have different statuses.

A possible consequence of this view is that there are an infinite number of statuses when we consider the infinite number of reference groups possible. This is true theoretically, but such a relativistic result would be chaotic for purposes of prediction and is not likely in actuality for two reasons. 1. The number of reference groups habitually used by individuals (as in the interview study) is relatively small despite the huge number of reference groups theoretically available. 2. Despite the large number of possible reference groups, it is likely that particular reference groups are specified by or are relevant to particular problems of status, *e.g.*, if a woman goes for a job as a model and her physical attractiveness is the desideratum, it may be irrelevant to the situation what her physical attractiveness is in relation to her friends, Hottentot women, etc. The relevant reference group is composed of the available women models. Furthermore, the variable of reference group may be manipulated systematically. With certain additional data, it is likely that the direction and the amount of shift in status can be predicted when two different reference groups are used, providing the relations of the two reference groups are known.

LITERATURE

No studies on subjective status as a function of reference groups or individuals were found. Many studies, however, indicate the potency of the frame of reference in judgment. Lewin (43) states that "judgment, understanding, perception are impossible without a related background and the meaning of every event depends directly upon the nature of its background," although the background itself is not often perceived. Lewin continues and discusses the social group to which the subject belongs in the light of a frame of reference. He states that one of the most important constituents of the ground is the social group of which the individual is a member. The same individual generally belongs to many groups and the importance of particular membership in a given group varies from time to time and in different situations.

Uncertainty about belonging may result from standing near a margin of two groups. With little extension this statement applies to our discussion of reference group and status. Similarly, Sherif (72) states, "throughout the major psychological phenomena in judgment, perception, memory, affectivity, it has been observed that data are definable only in relation to a frame of reference." Gordon Allport (2) suggests that the concept of frame of reference will enable us to make serviceable prediction concerning individual happenings. Experimental instances of the effect of the frame of reference interpreted in terms of anchoring of the absolute scale have been reported by Volkmann (80) and Rogers (66) for psychophysical judgments of visual inclination, by Volkmann and Hunt (33) for affective judgments, and by Chapman and Volkmann (14) for level of aspiration. McGregor (53) and Cantril (10) have analyzed predictive judgments in the light of the concept. Asch, Block, Hertzman (5) have indicated the effect of the introduction of arbitrary standards on rankings of photographs, professions, political figures, and political slogans.

The experiment discussed below, in which the reference group was the independent variable, was designed to demonstrate some of the lawful relations between change in the reference group and judgments of status.

Procedure

The procedure has been described in the discussion of reliability and construction of the scale. Each status was judged in each of three specified reference groups and thus we have three "values" of the independent variable. Changes in certain of the estimates of status are a consequence of changing the reference group.

Subjects

The subjects number 80, 48 men and 32 women. None of these subjects had been used in the interview study. These subjects included all those who were used in the reliability calculations plus additional subjects. Thirty-four were married, forty-four single, and two were divorced or widowed. Twenty-one had some degree of college training, fifty-two had had only high school educations or technical training, and the highest formal education for the remaining seven subjects was elementary school. Age and income distributions follow:

TABLE 9
AGES AND INCOMES OF THE SUBJECTS IN THE REFERENCE GROUP EXPERIMENT

Age	Frequency	Income	Frequency
17–20	23	0– 499	4
21–24	23	500– 999	22
25–28	9	1000–1499	17
29–32	2	1500–1999	5
33–36	3	2000–2499	5
37–40	10	2500–2999	5
41–44	5	3000–3499	4
45–48	1	3500–3999	3
49–52	1	4000–4499	4
Unspecified	3	4500–4999	1
	—	5000–5499	4
	80		
		7000–7999	1
		8000–plus	2
		Unspecified	3
			—
			80

The occupations represented and their frequencies were: 26 housewives, 9 in machine or mechanical work, 12 clerks, 5 in business, 2 chauffeurs, 2 engineers, and one in each of the following occupations: secretary, editorial writing, shoe production, errand work, student, salesgirl, seaman, waiter, embroiderer, tailor, office boy, factory worker, laundry worker, furrier, wireman, typesetter, social work, technician, assistant in college. Five subjects did not specify their occupations.

RESULTS AND DISCUSSION OF RESULTS

Four major alterations in subjective status are produced by changing the independent variable of reference group.

1. *The Experimental Production of Changes in Status*

Within each status dimension an individual's judgment of his status shifts when reference groups are changed. These results are presented in Table 10 and were worked out as follows: A. The shift in each subject's judgment, irrespective of sign, when a reference group was changed was calculated. This shift was determined for all three possible changes of reference groups, total population to occupation, total population to friends, and occupation to friends. B. The mean shift was then determined for the total male and female populations for each dimension of status and all three possible changes of reference groups. C. The mean of these three mean shifts was then calculated, and is an expression of the degree of experimental change when *any* reference group is substituted for any other.

TABLE 10

MEAN SHIFT IN STATUS AS A FUNCTION OF CHANGE IN THE REFERENCE GROUP

	General	Economic	Intellectual	Cultural	Social	Attractiveness
			Men, N = 48			
Total—occupation	18.8*	18.45	17.65	16.57	12.54	10.15
Total—friends	17.09	16.30	15.56	18.02	14.93	10.24
Occupation—friends	23.91	16.68	22.21	18.77	12.43	12.31
Mean of 3	19.93	17.14	18.47	17.79	13.30	10.90
Mean shift Sigma mean	9.11	7.20	7.73	6.13	5.54	5.00
			Women, N = 32			
Total—occupation	17.00	13.36	17.71	15.54	13.84	15.06
Total—friends	14.93	12.81	14.67	13.29	12.72	9.5
Occupation—friends	14.10	11.03	14.48	8.37	12.56	14.87
Mean of 3	15.34	12.40	15.62	12.40	13.04	13.14
Mean shift Sigma mean	7.48	4.56	7.23	5.61	5.11	5.62

* The amounts of shift are given in terms of the units of the status scale. The scale contained 100 units.

All the shifts are large, ranging from 10.15 to 23.91 for men, and 9.5 to 17.71 for women. It was necessary, however, to determine whether these mean shifts were significantly greater than chance. The significance of difference between means could not be used since the mean shift without regard to sign is not the same as the difference between means. Furthermore, since the shifts are in both directions and are about of equal magnitude they cancel each other out in the means. For each sample the mean of the judgments for each status using the total population as a reference group was calculated; the sigma of this mean was also calculated. The mean shift when any two reference groups were interchanged was compared with the sigma of this mean by "critical ratio." The logic was as follows: If the mean shift is 3 times as great as the sigma of the mean, it would indicate that the experimental shift is significantly greater than the maximum change that would occur in the mean of the judgments by chance.

These "CRs" range from 4.55 to 9.11. Consequently, all the shifts in status are significant. This is an experimental demonstration that the reference group is a variable of importance in determination of status, and considerable care should be used in the future in specifying the appropriate reference group in measuring status.

Although the direction of shift is an important problem, the preliminary problem is to demonstrate the phenomenon of experimental shifts in status irrespective of direction. Furthermore, in order to predict the direction of shift, it is necessary to know the relative statuses of the two reference groups in addition to the individual's status within the reference groups. This problem would demand a whole series of additional judgments of the status of the reference groups, and it was not feasible to tax the subjects with an additional task. It is inadequate to infer the relations of the reference groups from their objective differences since that would commit the fallacy of confusion between objective and subjective status, e.g., despite the fact that a person's occupational group is objectively lower in economic status than his friends, his "psychological environment" may be so organized that he does not regard this to be the case.

2. *Interrelations between Statuses and the Reference Group*

It was thought that certain status dimensions would be interrelated. Two logical clusters of status are intellectual and cultural status, and social and economic status. High social status is often thought to be a function of high economic standing, and a person of high intellectual status has probably high cultural standing because of the similarity of the two dimensions. It seemed likely, however, that changing the reference group would change the degree of relatedness of the dimensions for two reasons: 1. Experimental: Asch, Block, and Hertzman (5) have indicated experimentally that the introduction of reference points for the judgment of one trait alters the correlation between judgments of that trait and other traits. The introduction of such points operates to redefine the object of judgment. Therefore judgments of other traits for this object of judgment are affected. Hertzman (30) has indicated that specific alterations in the judgment situation by the introduction of reference points have general effects. The reference point affects parts of the judgment situation on which no direct influence has been brought. 2. Logical: The relatedness of two statuses is due to the fact that the individual or group judges the two statuses on the basis of criteria or achievements common to both. Such a common ground may be accepted by one reference group, and in another reference group the determination of the two statuses may be based on independent criteria. For example, among psychologists a man's intellectual status may be a function of scientific achievement or theoretical ability, and whether he is cultured or not does not affect his intellectual status. In the eyes of the total population, the two statuses may be linked. This argument, however, assumes some interiorization of the attitudes of the group since it is the individual who is making the judgments and not the group. If the individual had some stable level of "self regard" or if his judgments did not reflect the group which was specified or in which he operated, no changes should be found.

Data on experimental changes in the degree of relatedness are presented in Table 11 for male and female populations. The judgments of intellectual and cultural status, and social and economic status were correlated for the total population and occupational reference groups.

TABLE 11

INTERCORRELATIONS BETWEEN STATUSES AS A FUNCTION OF THE REFERENCE GROUP

	Economic and Social		Intellectual and Cultural	
	Male	Female	Male	Female
Total population	.24	.06	.78	.66
Occupation	.35	.22	.46	.75

The significance of difference between these correlation coefficients was calculated by the use of Fisher's Z correlation function. The samples available for the tests of significance, however, were not independent, and consequently the likelihood of significance is reduced by the lack of a measure of the dependence of the samples.

Of the four changes in the intercorrelation between statuses as a function of the reference group, only one is significant, *i.e.*, intellectual and cultural status for male subjects when the reference group is changed from total population to occupation. The difference of .32 is significant at the 1% level. None of the other

TABLE 12

CRITICAL RATIOS FOR THE SIGNIFICANCE OF THE DIFFERENCE BETWEEN INTERCORRELATION COEFFICIENTS

	Economic and Social		Intellectual and Cultural	
	Male	Female	Male	Female
CR for the difference between the total population and occupation intercorrelations	.60	.63	2.74*	.64

	T–values	
	5%	1%
N = 29	2.04	2.76
N = 45	2.02	2.69

* Significant difference at the 1% level.

changes (.09, .11, .16) is significant and it is questionable whether the introduction of a correlational term (for the lack of independence of the samples) would raise these values to the level of significance. It is shown, however, that significant changes in relatedness can be produced by alteration of the reference group since one such change was found.

The degree of relatedness between statuses is an interesting datum. Intellectual and cultural status correlate highly in three instances, which is to be expected. A surprising finding is the negligible relation between social and economic status despite the usual view of high correspondence. It may be correctly argued that the degree of relatedness is a function of the way the dimensions were defined, and that by changing the commonness of the criteria any degree of relatedness may be produced. The result, however, cannot be disputed in such fashion since the criteria for the definitions were those spontaneously reported in the interview study. People habitually defined social and economic status in the terms of the study, and within the limitations of the sample the low intercorrelation is a valid expression of the degree of relationship. This low intercorrelation between social and economic status is supported to some extent by the cultural lag between accorded social status and objective economic status. For example, a person who becomes rich achieves high objective economic status long before he is accorded high social status; he is a member of the *nouveau riche*. The impoverished aristocrat, on the other hand, maintains high accorded social status despite low objective economic status.

A feature of the relation between social and economic status is the consistent tendency to report social status as higher than economic status. This is true for both male and female subjects and for both the total population and occupational reference groups. Mean values are presented in Table 13 to indicate the trend. Critical ratios indicate that these differences are significant.

TABLE 13
THE RELATION BETWEEN SOCIAL AND ECONOMIC STATUS

	Total Population		Occupation	
	Male	Female	Male	Female
Mean economic status	58.46	57.74	50.21	52.50
Mean social status	66.29	68.88	64.48	60.34
CR for the difference between social & economic status	2.52	3.08	4.53	2.06
Probability	99	99+	99+	98

There are two possible interpretations of the result: 1. The finding may represent the intrinsic relation between the two dimensions, *i.e.*, social status is determined in this fashion by one's economic status. 2. Social status is a medium of compensation for economic status.

The finding and the second interpretation of it are supported by unpublished data of Cantril (12) on subjective class-identification. The relationship between social and economic class may be inferred from the percentage of individuals who identify themselves with a social class higher than the economic class they identified with. Forty-two and five tenths percent of the total sample reported their social class as one or more steps higher than their economic class. If it can be shown that this discrepancy is differentially characteristic of the people who identified themselves as of the low economic class, it suggests that the phenomenon represents a compensation in the social status sphere for low economic status. Tables indicate this.

TABLE 14
THE PERCENT OF GIVEN ECONOMIC CLASSES WHO REPORT THEIR SOCIAL CLASS ONE OR MORE CLASSES HIGHER THAN THEIR ECONOMIC CLASS

Economic Class	Percent of Class
Lower	73
Lower middle	71.6
Middle	12.6
Upper middle	7.4

TABLE 15

THE PERCENT OF GIVEN ECONOMIC CLASSES WHO REPORT THEIR SOCIAL
CLASS ONE STEP HIGHER THAN THEIR ECONOMIC CLASS

Economic Class	Percent of Class
Lower	15.1
Lower middle	62.1
Middle	8.2
Upper middle	7.4

These data were worked out by calculating what percent of the people of given subjective economic classes said they were of a social class one or more classes higher than their economic class. The differences strongly suggest the compensation theory, but there may be an artefact due to restriction of the scale in that there are fewer classes above one as one goes up in the economic structure. Therefore, the same procedure was repeated for each economic class and the percent of the class who said that were only one class higher was calculated since all classes have at least one available class above them. The data show that such a process is characteristic essentially of the groups, identifying with the low and lower middle economic classes and the difference between these two classes indicates that the low class tends to raise its social class more than one step higher whereas the lower middle people tend to raise themselves only one-step to the middle class level.

The results might, also, be interpreted as a function of regression toward the mean. In such a case the low and lower middle classes would report their social class higher. The low class would have to regress more to reach the mean producing a situation of differential enhancement of social status. This explanation is unsatisfactory in view of the results plotted in Figure 2. Regression toward the mean would demand that the upper economic classes report their social class lower in as great a percentage of cases as the lower economic classes move upwards. The data do not indicate such a situation. In Figure 2 such "regression" is plotted. Only 38% of the upper economic class and 24% of the upper middle class report their social class lower than their economic, while 73% and 71% of the low and lower middle economic classes report their social class higher.

3. *The Reliability of Judgments as a Function of the Reference Group*

The reliability coefficients reported in Chapter III (Tables 8, 8a,

56   THE PSYCHOLOGY OF STATUS

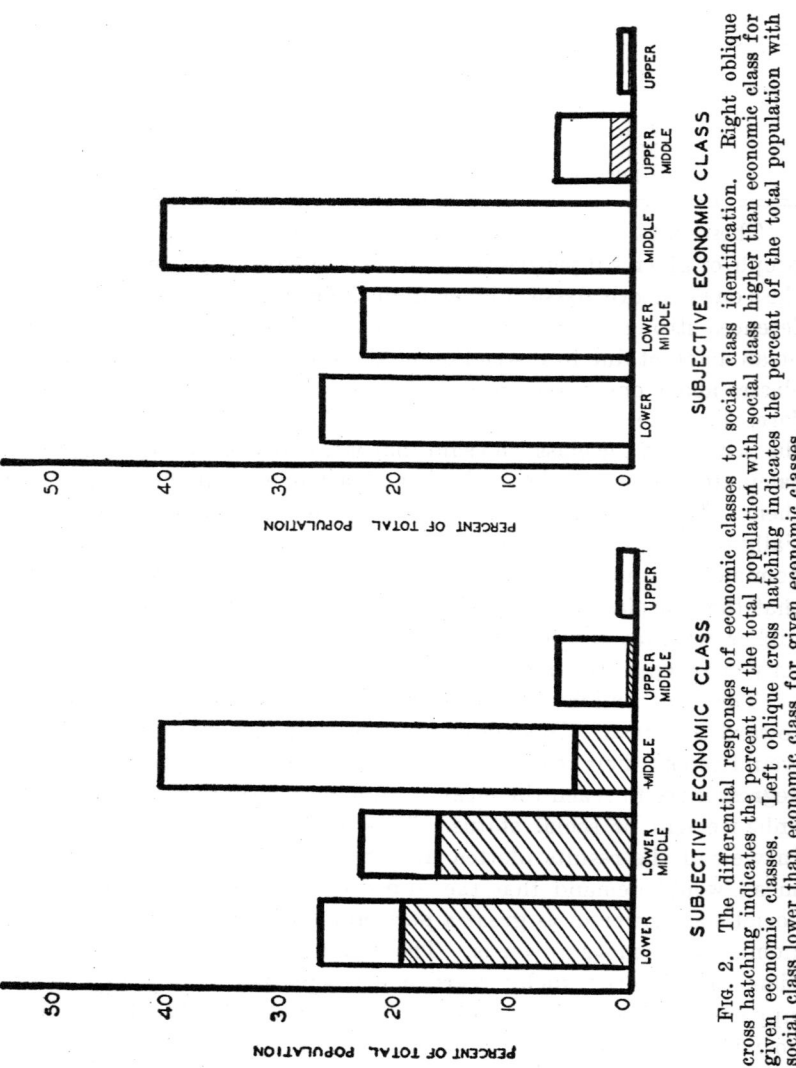

FIG. 2. The differential responses of economic classes to social class identification. Right oblique cross hatching indicates the percent of the total population with social class higher than economic class for given economic classes. Left oblique cross hatching indicates the percent of the total population with social class lower than economic class for given economic classes.

p. 44) for the scales used in this study are a function of the reference group, as has been pointed out. Graphic instances of this tendency are noted in the reliability coefficients of the male population. Economic status is judged reliably only in relation to the occupational group and the coefficients for the other two reference groups are not significantly greater than zero. Similarly, social status is judged with some degree of reliability only in relation to the reference group of friends and the reliabilities for the other two reference groups are not significantly greater than zero. Consequently, if one wishes to measure a given subjective status reliably, one must specify the most adequate reference group. It is certainly striking that most objective measures of economic status are concerned with position in relation to the total population reference group which is the least adequate of the three groups used in this study.

4. *The Relation of General Status to the Reference Group*

The "composition" of general status is a function of the reference group. The nature of this finding will be reserved for the following chapter, which is devoted entirely to a treatment of general status.

SUMMARY

The introduction of a systematic change in the reference group alters judgments of status in four ways: 1. Changes in an individual's status are experimentally produced. 2. The interrelation between statuses may be altered. 3. The reliability of subjective status is a function of the reference group, and 4. The composition of general status varies with the reference group specified.

CHAPTER V

THE COMPOSITION OF GENERAL STATUS WITH REFERENCE TO THE ROLE OF VALUES

Linton (46) has defined general status as the sum total of all the specific statuses the individual occupies. This experiment was designed to see what the characteristics of subjective general status were. The results of the interview study suggest certain findings which may be relevant to the problem.

INTERVIEW FINDINGS

1. General status was rarely reported spontaneously in the interview material. Only twelve out of the thirty-one subjects reported the dimension. This would suggest that possibly the concept is a logical construct rather than a psychological reality for most people. Nevertheless, individuals were able to make reliable judgments of their general status in relation to the total population and the occupational reference groups, despite the amorphous definition used in the study for general status. Apparently, despite the fact that the dimension may not be in the individual's spontaneous repertory, the judgment can be made.

2. In its historical development status is specific. If general status exists in the experience of individuals, it must develop late or on the basis of the combination of specific statuses.

3. A few subjects in the interview study not only reported general status, but also the criteria by which it was judged. The criteria shed some light on the composition of general status. These subjects (5 in number) reported criteria which were not unique; the criteria had already been used for specific dimensions of status. In four of the subjects, however, the criterion was from *one* specific status, which would most closely approximate intellectual status; the other subject said the dimension was a composite of the other statuses. Consequently, general status, in most of these cases, is not distinguishable from one specific status. Therefore, general status may not be a combination of *all* specific statuses as Linton suggests.

4. The relation of values to general status may be noted in certain of the protocols: Case #27 has a general dimension of status for which the reference group includes all people with whom she comes in contact. She states that economic and social status have

little to do with general status, while cultural and intellectual status are most important in determining it. She ranks cultural and intellectual status as second in importance among seven statuses, and economic status as least important. Case #18 thinks that general status is some sort of composite in which certain specific statuses are more important than others. Case #22 states that she has thought of a basic way by which people should be measured; the criteria are, however, intangible. This general dimension is certainly not based on economic or intellectual status alone, since the subject has felt superior to some individuals who have had higher intellectual or economic status than she. Consequently economic and intellectual status may either have no weight or little weight in determining general status. Case #19 reports that judgments of general status are immediate unitary products rather than *consciously* constructed composites.

The author made the following assumption on the basis of these data: Where general status can be judged, it represents some integration of more specific statuses. Furthermore, the data suggest that certain statuses may be important in the composition of general status, while others may not be. The amount of contribution of a specific status may be a function of the degree to which the individual values it.

The suggestion that values may enter into general status is also supported by experimental evidence on the generality of values. Cantril (9) and Cantril and Allport (13) report the generality of values, including such "modalities" as interest in clothes, one's conception of contentment, one's conception of the ideal person, one's conception of a leader, etc. Their findings suggest that values are generalized tendencies with important relations in conduct. Consequently, the generality may extend to subjective status.

An experiment was designed to determine the composition of general status and the role which values play in its formation.

Procedure

The study was included in the experimental session devoted to the determination of the effect of the reference group on judgments of status. All subjects judged their general status *first*, and then their five specific statuses. The judgments were made for each of the three reference groups. Three additional tasks were introduced *after* the judgments of status were made, in order to have a measure of the values of the specific statuses. They were:

1. The subjects ranked the five specific statuses in the order of their importance to them. The question was phrased thus:

> Listed below are five kinds of standing. I want to find out how important each of these is to you. The standing that means most to you, the one in which you would like to be highest, should be marked #1, the next most important #2, etc.

                       Rank
       Economic _____
       Intellectual _____
       Social _____
       Cultural _____
       Physical Attractiveness _____

The concept of importance was defined in this special fashion for the following reason: A very poor individual might be constrained to say economic standing is the most important to him since he lacks the necessities of life. Actually, he may not value economic status as highly as other statuses, but his condition of need would produce such an answer to the question of importance. However, given an adequate economic status, such a subject might prefer to raise other statuses. Therefore the qualification: "the one in which you would like to be highest" was introduced. The qualification permits such subjects to mark economic status with a low value despite its necessary importance. (This consideration applies to other statuses besides the economic which is offered only as an example.)

2. Cantril's Scale A for the study of values (9) was also administered so as to get a general values profile for the individual. This test was used instead of the Allport-Vernon scale (3) because of its brevity; it also has adequate reliability (r's range from .81 to .94).

3. The subjects were also asked to answer the following questions:

> You recall that you judged your general standing on pages 3-5. Look back and make sure you remember what general standing means. When you considered your general standing did you include any other standings than the ones listed immediately above (the five specific ones judged)? If so, write down the other standings you included.

SUBJECTS

The same 80 subjects were used in this study as in the reference group experiment. The data of only 61 subjects are presented, 36 men and 25 women. The remaining cases were omitted because they used additional statuses (other than the ones specified) in the judgment of general status. Such cases might show large errors because there would be no available measure of the additional specific statuses. These large errors would not mean that general status is not a composite. It might still be a composite and such errors would merely be a function of the lack of an available measure of all the components. Hence, the data of these subjects could not be used to test the theory of the composite nature of general status.

RESULTS

If general status represents a composite of specific statuses, in which all statuses are *equally* contributory irrespective of their values, the arithmetic mean of the specific statuses should approximate the empirical judgment of general status. Consequently, for each individual the arithmetic mean of his specific statuses was compared with his judgment of general status, and the difference between the two measures was considered the "error of prediction" based on this theory. The judgments of status in relation to both the total population and occupation reference groups were treated in this fashion. The experimenter computed the mean errors within each of the reference groups and compiled a frequency distribution of errors for the 61 subjects. The data are shown in Table 16 and

TABLE 16

THE DISCREPANCY BETWEEN A COMPOSITE SCORE OF EQUALLY WEIGHTED SPECIFIC STATUSES AND AN EMPIRICAL JUDGMENT OF GENERAL STATUS

Discrepancy*	Frequency	
	Total population	Occupation
0	1	2
1– 4	24	8
5– 8	14	15
9–12	6	8
13–16	7	6
17–20	3	5
21–24	2	5
25–28	1	8
29–32	2	1
33–36	1	1
37–40	0	2
	61	61
	Mean error	
Total population	8.56	
Occupation	13.89	

* The discrepancies are given in terms of the units of the status scale. The scale contained 100 units.

Figures 3 and 4. The reliability of judgments of general status in relation to the reference group of friends was not significantly greater than zero. Therefore, these data were not considered.

The significance of the difference between the two means could not be tested since the data are markedly skewed, the curves being

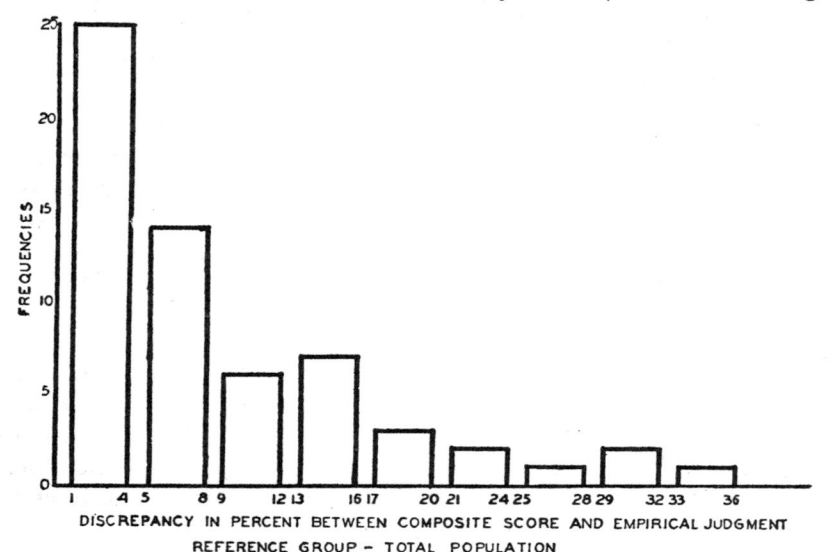

FIG. 3. The discrepancy between a composite score of equally weighted specific statuses and an empirical judgment of general status. (Reference group—total population.)

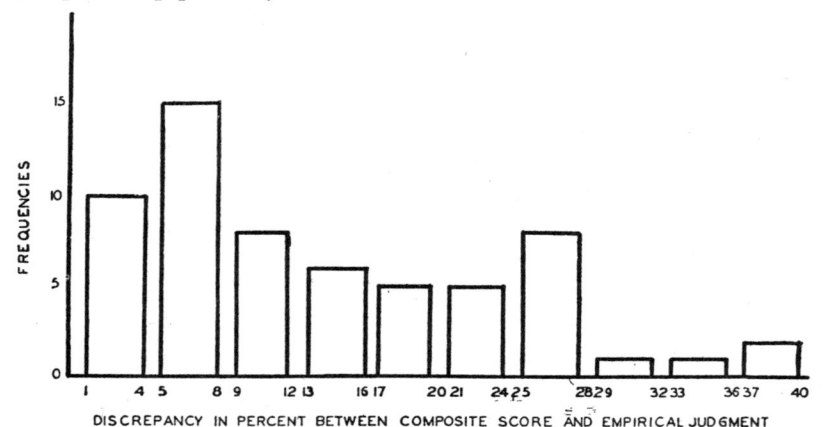

FIG. 4. The discrepancy between a composite score of equally weighted specific statuses and an empirical judgment of general status. (Reference group—occupation.)

J-shaped. Therefore the sigmas are not meaningful. Hence, the difference between the two distributions was tested by Chi-square. The distributions are significantly different at the 5% level.

Discussion of Results

For the total population reference group there is a relatively small error of prediction when equally weighted specific statuses are used. The mean error is about 9% (the errors are percent values since the scale has 100 points). However, the mean obscures the exceedingly fine prediction in many cases. The distribution of errors indicates that in 25 cases the error is 4% or less. Therefore, the composition of general status with the total population as a reference group seems to be a sum total of statuses as Linton suggests. This result tends to validate our choice of specific statuses since there would be large errors if the specific statuses chosen were not the relevant ones.

For the occupational reference group the mean error is considerably larger when equal weights are given to the specific statuses, and the two distributions are significantly different. Hence, the composition of general status seems to be a function of the reference group used. Why is prediction less adequate in the case of the occupational reference group?

The explanation probably lies in the fact that personal values may be an essential variable in general status when smaller reference groups are specified. Within the total population the values which specific statuses have are equivocal. No one status is the most important. Within the occupational group, however, one specific status may be unequivocally emphasized and contribute maximally to general status while other statuses are less important or bear no weight. For example, among psychologists, intellectual status may be most important in one's general standing, and attractiveness may play a small part or none at all. This argument assumes, however (as pointed out in Chapter IV), some interiorization of the attitudes of the group, since it is the individual who makes the judgments and not the reference group. It is also possible that some members of given occupations may accept and interiorize the values of their group while other people have their own atypical values despite membership in the group.

The crucial test of the hypothesis would be to give differential weights to the specific statuses and to note that prediction is enhanced in the occupational reference group and not in the total

population reference group. Weights may be derived from the profile of values and used for this purpose. The experimenter intended to follow this procedure, but there are numerous difficulties:
1. The rank order of values of the statuses is inadequate for the determination of differential weights. It is an intensive scale and although one status is more highly valued than another, the difference in magnitude of the values cannot be inferred. 2. The Cantril scale may be used, but this also has difficulties. This scale is probably intensive also. It is questionable whether the scale numbers have arithmetic properties, *i.e.*, a theoretical value of 12 may not be twice as strong as an economic value of 6. Also, there are no apposite values for certain of the statuses used. There is no apposite value for attractiveness-status, nor is the "social" value defined in terms of social status as used in this study. Another difficulty is that the choice of differential weights is arbitrary and may result in errors of prediction.

4. The values desirable for the determination of the differential weights may be either the *personal* profile or the *occupational* profile. Where individuals have adopted the values of their group there will be no discrepancy between their personal profile and the typical occupational profile. Where individuals have values different from the typical values of their group, it is a question which set of values should be used for the choice of weights. In such instances the values perhaps should be those general for most of the people in the given occupation, since the contributions of the statuses seem to be specified by the nature of the reference group. Cowdery (15), Mallory (50), Duffy and Crissy (18), Allport and Vernon (3), Pintner (16), and Harris (25) have already indicated such occupational and group differences in values. Such occupational profiles might be used, or an occupational profile might be determined in a manner analogous to the determination of occupational profiles of abilities (36).

For all these reasons the answer to the problem can only be tentative. With the development of transitive scales for the measurement of values, the hypothesis may be substantiated by differential weighting. While the ideal procedure of deriving weights is not possible, the theory may be tentatively tested by other methods:

1. A possible interpretation of the data is that certain individuals have stable systems of strongly contrasted values, and that for such individuals general status may always reflect the role of

values *whatever the reference group*. This suggestion is amenable to test. The eleven cases in which there were the largest errors (25% or more) in the occupational reference group were used. The mean error of prediction for the occupational reference group was compared with the mean error for the total population reference group. The results are presented in Table 17.

TABLE 17

THE CORRESPONDENCE BETWEEN ERRORS OF PREDICTION IN THE TWO REFERENCE GROUPS FOR THE ELEVEN SUBJECTS WHO SHOWED THE LARGEST ERRORS IN THE OCCUPATIONAL REFERENCE GROUP

Reference Group	Mean
Occupation	29.91
Total population	7.73

If the errors were merely due to certain individuals whose contrasting values demanded differential weighting, such individuals would show large errors in both reference groups. The data do not support this view. Large errors for these people seem to occur only in the presence of the occupational reference group.

2. Whether or not the values enter the picture when brought into play by the occupational reference group may be inferred by contrasting the profiles of these individuals who show large errors with those who show small errors of prediction for the occupational reference group. The range of possible scores on the values test is 0–12. The difference between the strongest and the weakest of the three apposite values was calculated for twelve individuals for whom there were complete profiles: a group of 8 subjects who showed errors of 25% or more, and a group of 4 subjects who showed errors of 4% or less.

TABLE 18

THE DIFFERENCE BETWEEN THE STRONGEST AND WEAKEST OF THREE APPOSITE VALUES FOR GROUPS WITH CONTRASTING ERRORS OF PREDICTION

Group	Mean Difference in Units of the Cantril Scale
Large errors of prediction	7.5
Small errors of prediction	3.0

These results strongly suggest that values play a role in general status when brought into operation by a given reference group.

Those individuals with small differences between values should show small errors (in occupational judgments) since relatively little differential weighting would be needed; those subjects with large differences between values should show large errors of prediction since much differential weighting would be needed.

A possible criticism that might be leveled against the "prediction" is that it is an artefact which is a function of a constant judgment of status, *e.g.*, a given subject might judge all his statuses as 50; and hence there would be no error. The answer is clear on several grounds: 1. The intercorrelations between given statuses are not high, as would be the case if there was a constant level of judgment for each individual subject. 2. In the experimental procedure, general status could not be judged on the basis of the actual judgments of the specific statuses, since it was judged first. General status was defined, also, in a neutral manner. The Experimenter did this so as not to *indicate* the composite nature of general status. Consequently, the composite nature of the dimension is not a function of the definition. 3. The determination of general status is not direct. Scoring of the judgment involves adding $\frac{1}{2}$ the middle category to the lower judgment. It would be exceedingly difficult for the subject to have a constant status when the index of status is this measure. 4. The empirical fact is that there is no constant level of status judgments. The range of judgments for the 6 statuses was calculated for all male subjects, for all three reference groups, and is reported below:

TABLE 19
THE MEAN RANGE OF JUDGMENTS OF ALL SIX STATUSES

	Mean
Total population	32.12
Friends	32.43
Occupation	39.54

SUMMARY

The findings suggest that general status represents a composite of specific statuses. The nature of this composite is a function of the reference group which may act to bring into operation the values characteristic of the individual or the group. In such instances, it is tentatively indicated that specific statuses contribute to general status in accordance with their degree of value.

CHAPTER VI

STATUS AND ATTITUDES

The preceding chapters have been devoted to an analysis of some of the properties of subjective status. This chapter is concerned with the relation of subjective status to attitudes. The writer has limited this part of the study to Radical-Conservative attitudes concerning economic issues.

LITERATURE

The large number of investigations on the relation of objective status and radicalism implies that many writers believe status to be an important variable. The essentially negative findings of most of these studies are reported below. This writer feels that status is a variable in the determination of attitudes, but that appropriate measures of status may not have been used. Consequently, a demonstration of the relation of subjective measures of status to attitudes would offer new hope to any theory of the relation of status and attitudes.

Consequently, the author has reviewed the relevant literature on the problem, limiting the treatment to studies of economic radicalism. A major limitation of some of the attitude studies is that most of the subjects have been college undergraduates. This is a limiting circumstance for two reasons: 1. College graduates represent a small and selected proportion of the total population (12% approximately) and there is little information on the mass of non-college people. 2. Students for the most part, have equivocal status. They have the vicarious status of their parents as well as their own or potential status, *e.g.*, the very fact that the sons of laborers are in college means that they no longer are representative of the laboring class; the son of a banker with a future career as a laboratory technician will not be representative of the banking class; students have not realized an independent status yet, in that they are not earning a living or have few problems of expenses and dependents. Consequently, the conclusions of such studies may not be very significant.

In analyzing the data it was felt that the operation of objective status should reflect itself in the following ways:

1. Significant differences should be found between objectively different income or occupational groups. These differences should be in a direction logically consistent with some theoretical inter-

pretation, *i.e.*, the fact that bankers' sons are significantly more radical than laborers' sons would not support the usual view of the relation of low income and radicalism. F. H. Allport (1) is an exponent of a prevailing theory. He states that radicalism represents a rationalization for attitudes of inferiority associated with poverty. Poverty is seen as an injustice of the social order rather than as a consequence of personal inferiority. Thus, the radicals are usually the have-nots, while the conservatives belong to the propertied classes.

2. Some degree of uniformity should obtain within a given income or occupational class. If objective status is the determinant of radicalism, people of the same objective status should show similar attitudes. Hence there should be uniformity. If the group is not uniform, it implies the operation of another variable such as subjective status, or heterogeneity in respect of geographical region, sex, nationality, personality, etc.

The following studies are relevant to the issue:

1. *Studies Using Traditional Attitude Scales Where Objective Status Is Not Significant*

1. Rosenthal (68) administered two attitude scales to college students. Students were divided into three occupational classes on the basis of father's occupation: a. propertied, b. non-propertied, c. professional. Classes a and b were not significantly different. The professionals were more conservative than the other classes. The critical ratios for the differences between the propertied and professional classes, and the non-propertied and professional classes were respectively 2.45 and 2.11. In this study objective status of the fathers is not a significant variable and the direction of the difference is not consistent with the view that wealth tends towards conservatism. When the attitudes are broken down according to content of items, none of the differences is reliable. When the groups are broken down into smaller occupational categories, the results are even more paradoxical, *e.g.*, manufacturers' sons are almost as radical as those of non-skilled laborers. Rosenthal concludes, in apparent contradiction to the data, that the broad socio-economic background contributed to radicalism. He argues, however, that the sons of the non-propertied classes in college are not representative, and therefore the data may not be definitive.

2. Gundlach (22) administered a scale of "politico-economic" radicalism to 290 students and analyzed the data according to fam-

ily income. In the radical group 25% had families with incomes below $1500 and 6% with incomes above $2500, whereas the conservative group reversed this income classification. This is suggestive of the view that low objective status produces radicalism, but 69% of both groups were in the same income class; hence the factor of income is none too relevant. However, Gundlach states that the vast majority of students show no consistency in their socioeconomic views, and if economic status were a major determinant this should not be the case except insofar as students have equivocal status.

3. Vetter (79) compared the mean family incomes of groups differentiated according to their attitudes. All groups from the radicals to the conservatives were in relatively high income levels, which makes the study none too conclusive. The fact of the high level of incomes, however, in itself works against a theory of the relation of low objective status and radicalism, *i.e.*, 60 "radicals" show a mean yearly income of $7109. No critical ratios are reported, but the differences according to Vetter seem significant. The direction of the differences is not consistent with any logical theory. While liberals and radicals have lower incomes than conservatives, the liberals (lowest income of all) have lower incomes than the radicals, and the reactionaries have lower incomes than the conservatives.

4. Lentz (42) compared the economic status of the 100 most radical and 100 most conservative subjects differentiated according to their responses to his C-R scale. The conservatives present a family background appreciably *lower* economically than the radicals *e.g.*, conservatives have 11% more fathers doing unskilled work, radicals have 13% more fathers and 13% more mothers doing professional work. Nevertheless, Lentz suggests that in other parts of the study (unpublished) conservatives are more capitalistic than radicals despite the above result.

5. Newcomb and Svehla (59) report data relevant to the problem. One of the attitude scales administered was a Thurstone scale towards Communism. Adult subjects in occupational levels 1, 2, 5, 6, (according to the Goodenough schema) are less favorable to Communism than adults in occupational level 4. The middle occupational level is least conservative. These data do not indicate a relation of low objective status and radicalism.

6. O. M. Hall (24) contrasted 300 employed engineers with 360 unemployed engineers during the depression when there was little

hope of re-employment. The groups were matched for age, etc. A 57-item scale included opinions on religion, employers, occupational morale, form of government, Communism, income, etc. The difference between the means of both groups was significant on attitudes towards employers, although the distributions greatly overlapped. Thirty-one out of the fifty-seven items, however, show no reliable difference. Hence, the mean difference conceals the inconsistency of the attitudes of the group, *i.e.*, they only differ on 26 items. Certainly, if objective status were important there should be more consistent differences with respect to all the items. It may be argued that the lack of difference in these 31 items is due to the fact that some of the items in any scale are not discriminative or reliable. Hence one should not expect differences on some items. This contention is not fair, however. Once a scale is constructed, and the reliability and the discriminative value of the items determined on a standardization group, one cannot fall back on this argument. If this argument were admissable, one could always explain away negative results. The experimenter who devises a scale and determines its reliability can no longer use the contention of unreliability at a later date. If the items are used, they should be assumed to be reliable. When we examine the percent of uniformity within each group, we find a lack of homogeneity. The author noted the number of items in which as little as 45–55% of a given group agreed on one opinion. Such responses indicate lack of uniformity, in that about half of the class has one opinion and the other half the contrasting opinion. In the unemployed, 15 attitude items received 45–55% of the responses in one direction, while in the employed 8 attitude items received 45–55% of the responses in one direction.

7. Murphy and Likert (57) state that economic status is a variable of small importance in understanding economic radicalism in their results. They report a very low correlation between income and economic radicalism on a college population. On retest, five years later, when the subjects were earning their own livings, the results are negative. There were no differences between the groups earning $1000–$1800, $1800 and more, and $1000 and less. The five unemployed subjects were similar in attitude to the employed.

2. *Studies Using Indices Other Than Attitude Scales in Which Low Economic Status Does Not Correspond with Radicalism*

1. Sorokin (74) compared the relative contributions of the various occupational classes (based on the Barr and Taussig classifica-

tion) to labor leadership. Assuming the percent of leaders to be an index of relative radicalism of a given class, we find: In examining the occupational status of the fathers of labor leaders, the percent from the unskilled and semi-skilled classes is 9.4%, 52.5% come from the skilled laboring, clerical, and small official classes, while 23.2% come from the professional, managerial, and business classes. These data are not a function of the proportion of that class in the total population since the upper classes contribute in great disproportion to their total numbers. Thus, it is wrong to conclude that labor leaders come from the lowest classes. These data suggest that low income groups contribute less to radicalism. There are two qualifications, however: A. The measure is probably not an appropriate index of radicalism and B. The relation may be a function of the greater education and superior opportunity for leadership in the higher classes. The occupational classes of the leaders themselves indicate that only 6% are from the lowest classes. This measure is inadequate since a labor leader of sufficient rank to be included in the 1925 *American Labor Who's Who,* of necessity would no longer be a member of the lowest working classes.

2. Willoughby (84) studied the problem by correlating the subscription figures to *The Nation* in various states as an index of relative radicalism with the number of taxable incomes per thousand native whites as an index of relative economic level. The correlation equalled + .51 and when urbanism is partialled out the r drops to + .35. This relationship is in a direction inconsistent with the usual view since it may be interpreted in terms of the more wealthy states being more radical. However, the relation may just reflect an increased ability of the wealthy to buy periodicals in general, and Willoughby suggests a comparative study of the subscriptions to an innocuous magazine.

3. Breslaw (8) studied by interview technique 47 conservatives and 47 radicals, all beyond working age, who were unequivocally conservative or radical according to their response to a single question concerned with changing the system of private enterprise. The mean incomes of the groups up to the time of the formation of the attitude were not significantly different. Where income was included in a cluster with other variables to note its effect in conjunction with other factors, it was effective in only one instance. Breslaw states that income has a much lower directive value than people suppose in the genesis of attitudes. Income is no more important than other single factors, and the only instances in which

it was important were those in which wealthy individuals, suddenly made poor, adopted a radical view.

3. *Studies with the Use of Attitude Scales in Which the Relation of Economic Status and Radicalism Is Equivocal*

1. Sims (73) analyzed the results of a questionnaire on the TVA with respect to occupational differences. Favorable attitude towards the TVA may be interpreted as the more radical point of view. The direction of the differences supports the idea that low economic status favors radicalism. The laboring and farm groups were most favorable, professionals next, and business and industry least favorable. The difference between the laboring and professional groups was not significant. This study for the most part indicates a relation between low objective status and radicalism. It is classified as equivocal only because the difference between the objectively defined laboring and professional groups was not significant.

2. Gundlach (23) administered a social attitudes scale to a large number of students and adults in which alternative answers represent shades of political opinion from reactionary to radical. The correlation for male subjects between income and radicalism was −.30, *i.e.*, the lower income groups were more radical and the trend is consistent. The group with incomes below $390 a year was reliably more radical than higher income groups. With respect to uniformity Gundlach states that this group was homogeneously radical! The group with incomes from $400 to $790 was reliably more radical than the groups above $1400. No other critical ratios are reported for the intermediate groups and if the r is only −.30, it would seem that the relation of radicalism to income at the higher levels is not very great. There were no reliable differences between any income groups for women subjects.

3. Mintzer and Sargent (55) administered a questionnaire on radical attitudes to a group of college students. The correlation between radicalism and low family status was .30 and the authors state that "apparently a bad family situation is only one of the many factors producing radicalism in college."

4. Harris, Remmers, and Ellison (26) report on the relation of occupational status of parents to scores on Harper's Liberalism-Conservatism questionnaire. The authors report that suggestive but unreliable differences in liberalism were found when students were grouped according to occupation of father. The direction of

the differences is peculiar. The semi-skilled were the most conservative. The professional group was not different from the skilled labor group.

G. A. Lundberg (48) reports a study using an index other than an attitude scale in which the relation between economic status and radicalism is equivocal. He compared radical and conservative communities in Minnesota and North Dakota using as an index of radicalism the relative support of the Non-Partisan League in the elections of 1916 to 1922. There were uniformly inferior economic conditions and greater economic insecurity in the radical counties. Radicalism, however, is not interpreted by Lundberg as intrinsic to low economic status. The correlation may represent selective migration of radicals to such counties. Also, the radical counties are regarded as underdeveloped and new communities. Radicalism is regarded as the attitude of the new, young, dynamic society. Both economic insecurity and freedom from social bonds which are characteristic of radicalism are a function of an early stage of community development. The results of this study are classified as equivocal since Lundberg qualifies the relation found.

4. *Studies Using Attitude Scales Where Objective Status Is Significant*

1. Kornhauser (38, 39, 41) in a number of studies reports status differences in attitudes. Complete data are not presented and hence the results are difficult to interpret. Data secured on 600 adults in Chicago indicate important differences for different income and occupational groups. Within each economic group those who express dissatisfaction differ significantly from those satisfied. This is especially true at the higher income levels; the difference at the lower income levels being less marked. Kornhauser reports almost as much dissatisfaction in the middle as in the low income groups in one study. The direction of the differences in attitudes between different economic groups is unfortunately not reported. The direction in which dissatisfied differ from satisfied is, also, not reported.

He also presents data which indicate that the differences between groups and the alignment of groups varies with the issues studied, *e.g.*, the middle income group agreed with the low on attitudes towards distribution of wealth and with the upper groups on unionism and socialization of industry. Thus, the agreement between objective classes is a function of the issues studied. For the most part there is a smooth gradient in the responses to the attitude items with no sharp cleavage from group to group. There are certain gaps, however. With respect to reform of the economic system there is a large jump from the $3000–$5000 class to the $5000 plus class. With respect to sympathies for labor the change in opinion is at the $3000 level. Most of the larger breaks are at $3000 and above, and this would imply that there are no psychologically distinct classes in the 80% of the population below this level.

Kornhauser also reviews a variety of public opinion studies concerned with radical attitudes, and reports marked differences correlated with objective differences in income as indicated by the percent of the different groups favoring a given point of view. The percent of uniformity within given groups, in many instances, is exceedingly high (90–100%). In other instances the percent of uniformity approximates 50% which suggests for these questions the inadequacy of the objective status variable. Some of this divergence of opinion, however, within a class may be a consequence of heterogeneity in respect of variables uncontrolled in the study.

2. Rundquist and Sletto (70) administered an attitude scale on economic radicalism to a population of 3000 cases. A sample of young unemployed individuals did not differ significantly from the employed groups. These unemployed lived with their parents and were not in great need economically. Their objective unemployment status did not truly reflect their relatively satisfactory position. When the sample was analyzed according to degree of certainty of maintaining employment (for the employed) and degree of certainty of obtaining employment for the unemployed, a significant relation was found. Those unemployed very uncertain of obtaining employment were most radical and the unemployed who were very certain of obtaining employment did not differ at all from the employed who were very certain of maintaining employment. Rundquist and Sletto, as well, found no relation of parental occupation to attitudes, and hence there is no use in classifying student attitude results according to occupational status of the parents. Similarly married men with dependents were consistently more radical than those without dependents. Thus unemployment affects subjects in accordance with the number of other "adverse" factors present.

In fifteen of the seventeen studies reviewed, the relation of economic status and radicalism is equivocal. In the two studies which report a relationship we note an approach in which the measurement of objective status is refined so as to yield significant results. Satisfaction is studied, the data are analyzed according to degree of security or need; classes are divided along functional lines according to the issues involved, etc. A relationship between objective status and attitudes does exist, but it will not be demonstrated by crude methods of status classification, which do not do justice to the personal facts. Murphy, Murphy and Newcomb suggest, "While many investigations include data on socio-economic status, most of them reveal no significant variations with attitude. It is probable that, in most cases, this is not because no such relationship exists, but rather that they have been concealed, in fact, doubly cloaked. Most of the measures of socio-economic status, in the first place, are based upon income, though such other considerations as occupational security, status, degree of organization, etc., are much more closely related to the processes by which attitudes are formed" (58). The writer would add subjective status as another important consideration in attitude formation, since subjective economic status does take account of just such criteria as relative need, source and security of income, dependents, likelihood of change of income, and standard of living. These are the factors which Murphy, Murphy and Newcomb regard as important and which were found to be important in the two successful studies cited.

5. *Subjective Status and Attitude Studies*

There are certain findings in the literature suggesting a relationship between subjective status and attitudes.

1. Holcombe (31) states that the middle class identification of the American people finds a correspondence in the attitudes revealed by the Fortune (78) survey. "For example, the majority of the people wish to go into business for themselves, a thoroughly middle class attitude. A majority desire success more than security, as revealed by their preference for a better position with an equal chance of advancement and of failure over an inferior position with little risk of dismissal. A majority favor private business over the government as an employer. A majority believe that the employer and worker go hand in hand together. This attitude is shared by all groups, including even factory workers. A majority believe that the future is still bright for themselves personally, and that opportunity for the advancement of one's children is greater than ever before. A majority have sent their children to college, or intend to do so, and a majority feel a sense of obligation to pass on something to the next generation. These are all middle class attitudes,

and could not exist unless the bulk of the people really were what they profess to be, members in spirit of the middle class."

2. Cantril's data (12) on attitudes towards taxation are broken down according to objective income groups and subjective class identification. The writer contrasted the two most distinct objective status groups (the groups earning respectively $15 or less a week and $60 or more a week). In only one of twelve comparisons is there a significant difference (at the 99% level) in the attitudes of the groups. When the data are analyzed according to subjective (social and economic) class identification, it is found that four out of fifteen tests of significance between the upper and lower subjectively defined classes are reliable at the 99% level.

Purpose of the Experiment

The analysis of the literature on objective economic status and radicalism has revealed that the relation found in most studies is negligible or equivocal. This experiment was designed to determine the relation between subjective status and radicalism.

Procedure

1. The scale of economic radicalism from the Minnesota Survey of Opinion (70) was administered to a group of subjects who had already made judgments of their status in the preceding study reported. Measures of subjective status and income, consequently, were available.

2. The scale was preceded by these additional instructions:

In answering any of these questions if your opinions have been affected by our entrance into the war, please answer them as you would have done previous to our entry into war.

3. The subjects were also asked to answer the question:

Are you in general satisfied with your present economic standing?

Subjects

There were 34 subjects, 18 women and 16 men. Thirteen had college educations, eighteen high school education. Eighteen were married and sixteen single. Age and income distributions follow:

The occupations represented and their frequencies follow: 15 housewives, 1 salesgirl, 3 clerks, 2 engineers, 4 in business, 1 social worker, 2 machinists, 1 college assistant, 1 embroiderer, 1 typesetter, 1 wireman. Two did not specify occupation.

TABLE 20
AGES AND INCOMES OF THE SUBJECTS IN THE ATTITUDE STUDY

Age	Frequency	Income	Frequency
17–20	5	500– 999	7
21–24	11	1000–1499	4
25–28	4	1500–1999	3
29–32	2	2000–2499	2
33–36	2	2500–2999	4
37–40	4	3000–3499	3
41–44	4	3500–3999	3
45–48	1	4000–4499	2
Unspecified	1	4500–4999	1
		5000–5499	3
		Unspecified	2

RESULTS

Correlations were calculated between the attitude scores and income, attitude scores and the three measures of subjective economic status (3 reference groups), and between the attitude scores and the three measures of subjective social status. These coefficients are reported in Table 21.

TABLE 21
THE CORRELATION BETWEEN ECONOMIC RADICALISM AND MEASURES OF OBJECTIVE AND SUBJECTIVE STATUS

	Subjective						Objective (income)
	Economic			Social			
	t*	f†	o‡	t	f	o	
Radical score	.10	.16	.06	.10	.26	.14	–.27
Significance of r, 32 degrees freedom, 5% level r = .349
1% level r = .449

* t = total population reference group.
† f = friends reference group.
‡ o = occupational reference group.

TABLE 22
THE RELATION BETWEEN RADICALISM SCORES AND SATISFACTION WITH ECONOMIC STATUS

	Mean Score
Satisfied group	65.33
Dissatisfied group	81.43
T-value, difference between means	2.02
T-table, 5% level of significance	2.08

The significance of the difference between the scores of the satisfied and dissatisfied groups as differentiated by item 3 in the procedure were calculated. These are reported in Table 22. The results border on significance at the 5% level.

Discussion of Results

None of the correlations is significantly different from zero. Hence, in this study the relation between measures of objective and subjective status and radical attitudes is negligible. The writer, however, feels that such a result is qualified by a number of factors.

1. The discriminative value of the test items can no longer be assumed. The opinions that formerly were characteristic of conservatives are no longer diagnostic. "The government should take over all large industries" was formerly answered in the negative by conservatives. The war situation today has transmuted the opinion into the affirmative for many conservative subjects. Similarly, some radicals may no longer agree that (in time of war) "A man should strike in order to secure greater returns to labor." Hence the negative results may be a function of the inability to get an appropriate measure of the attitude. This analysis is supported by the frequent questions of the subjects as to whether they should answer the test in the light of the present or as they would have formerly. The instructions prefaced to the scale were a makeshift to alleviate the situation. It is uncertain how well the subjects were able to abstract their opinions from the present life situation.

2. The sampling for the study did not include people of sufficiently diverse income or subjective status. There were no individuals in the really wealthy levels or in the lowest levels of the population. Consequently, lack of differences in radicalism may be truly representative of individuals so similarly placed in the status continuum. If groups with markedly different subjective or objective economic status were contrasted, however, differences in radicalism would probably be found.

3. The measures of subjective status used may not be the relevant ones for radical attitudes. Social status in the friends' reference group correlates more highly with radicalism than economic status or social status in the other reference groups. It is true that none of the correlation coefficients was significantly different from zero. The correlation for social status in the friends' reference group, however, bordered closest to the 5% level of significance. Perhaps another dimension of status in relation to other reference groups will show greater correspondence with radicalism.

There is a significant difference between satisfied and dissatisfied individuals on the attitude test. The dissatisfied are significantly more radical. As Kornhauser (41) has indicated, degree of satisfaction is an important correlate of attitudes, and such satisfaction is apparently elicited by the straightforward means of asking a direct question. The writer has pointed out that degree of satisfaction may not be inferred from mere objective or subjective status since factors of valuation of the dimension and aspiration enter.

SUMMARY

An analysis of the literature on objective status and radical attitudes reveals a negligible relation in most studies. A study of the relation between subjective status and radical attitudes was undertaken; the results are likewise negative. The correlations between measures of subjective status and radicalism are not significantly different from zero. Radicalism, however, is found to correspond with degree of satisfaction with economic status.

CHAPTER VII

IMPLICATIONS AND SUGGESTIONS FOR THE FUTURE

This chapter represents a speculative venture. The writer wishes to make certain suggestions for future research and to indicate a variety of possible problems which may be understood or clarified by a treatment in terms of subjective status. In many instances support for the statements may be found in the literature and such support will be cited.

The essential importance of the study lies not in its remote application but in the suggestion of a new methodology and a number of postulates in the realm of status. Insofar as problems of status may be regarded as important, this study is significant. Both by implication and statement, status has been thought of importance. In the work of Linton and others, we note its value in Ethnology; in Sociology work on problems of class stresses the concept; in the field of personality the recent books on the personality of Negro youth (16, 20, 34) stress the importance of status variables. In the understanding of attitudes, status has been considered a significant factor as indicated by many studies, some of which have been cited in Chapter VI. Variables such as the reference group, values, and the criteria for the determination of status should lead to further clarification of the field. The contrast between subjective and objective status and the emphasis on the subjective side, it seems to the writer, are worth emphasizing.

The variables of status are mediated through an individual who acts selectively in his choice of reference group, who strives selectively for status, whose personal values affect the composition of status and the emotional concomitants of a given status, whose conceptualization of a reference group may be different from its actual character, who is not affected by all aspects of the culture nor by all references in the environment. This essentially personal aspect of status cannot be ignored. We cannot deal with these variables independent of their meaning to individuals as has been done in the work on objective status. Lynd (49) states the case: "Understanding of institutions and social problems must be based upon analysis of what these institutions and problems *mean* to specific, differently situated people, how they look and feel to these different people, and how they are used."

Extensions of the study into wider fields of application may be indicated under four headings: 1. Direct outgrowths of the study; 2. Social implications; 3. Personality and adjustment; 4. Judgment and the frame of reference.

DIRECT OUTGROWTHS

1. The sampling should be broadened to include rural as well as urban people, other geographical areas, and people of more diverse and contrasted objective status.

2. If some satisfactory quantitative technique of measuring values becomes available, a further study of the relation of values to the composition of general status should be made.

3. Certain reference groups are probably most *relevant* to given situations, attitudes, or behavior. The problem of the choice of reference group for the determination of status should be investigated.

4. The attitude study should be repeated on a larger sample of more diverse objective economic status, using a scale that may be less affected by the present war situation. When judged against reference groups other than the ones used in this study, status may show a greater relation to attitude scores.

5. A study of the discrepancy between subjective status and accorded status would be of interest.

6. Sex and cultural differences in emphasis upon different statuses would be important to study. For example, cultural status might be more emphasized for women subjects in our society since culture has in part been stylized as a female virtue. Male beauty is emphasized in certain primitive societies, and a comparison between members of such societies and our society would yield significant data.

7. Aspects of status might be markedly different in a small city which offered individuals more common community membership than New York does. A community study on subjective status would be to the point.

8. A study of individuals with equivocal status would yield highly interesting results, *e.g.*, a study of youths, students, or marginal people who have group membership in several groups.

9. An actual genetic study of status in children would be an empirical way to get at the historical factors in the development of concepts of status.

10. A comparative study of subjective status in relation to class and caste societies should show certain findings. Where there is rigid formal status, there would probably be a small discrepancy

between objective and subjective status. Correspondingly, the departure of subjective from objective status in our society is a function of the *need* for such modes of adjustment for individuals with low status. This departure is made possible by the lack of rigid formal status. Hence, societies in which there is variation in stratification and mobility may show differences.

11. In acculturation studies, it would be interesting to note the degree of adoption of the dominant culture's status system and the conflict between an individual's status in one society and his status in the other. Such a study might be particularly interesting among politically "subject" peoples.

Social Implications

1. Personal correlates of cultural change and cultural lag: When an individual's objective status changes, his behavior should change in accordance with his new status. The failure of change in his behavior to correspond to the new status is a personal analogue of cultural lag. Part of the understanding of the phenomenon may lie in the fact that the individual's subjective status or class-identification has not changed and his behavior still mirrors this status. Such a phenomenon could be studied experimentally in a group of subjects whose objective situation has radically changed (for example, refugees). Subjective status could be elicited in the manner used in this study or in a similar manner. Such lag is not without purpose, nor does it always occur. Individuals probably do not adhere to former statuses of all sorts. The *nouveau riche* immediately assumes his new status and role, whereas the rich man made poor and the Southern aristocrat maintain their former subjective status. Probably, the old status operates where it provides greater ego enhancement than the new. Cantril (11) offers a suggestion for experimental approaches to this problem. In discussing the determinants of "suggestibility" he states that the more the self-enhancement produced by suggestion, the greater the likelihood that it will be accepted. This hypothesis could be demonstrated for subjective status. Two equally remote reference groups could be specified for the judgment of status, one which would tend to raise status and another which would tend to lower it. The relative effects could be determined. A field study, in which the actual situation was already arranged in this way, would be most desirable. Linton (46) mentions the problem briefly. He says that when an individual changes objective status, there may be a conflict between the status personalities for the former and the present roles.

Social change in its personal manifestations could be investigated. Two individuals whose objective statuses have changed and are now approximately equal, may have different interpretations of the change depending on the direction of the change. The person whose status has fallen may regard his subjective status differently from the person whose status has improved. The emotional consequences may be altogether different for the two individuals. To lump such people under one common category of status is to ignore the direction of change of status and its emotional accompaniments.

Cantril (11) discusses social change and suggests that where there is slow social change, it is indicative of the fact that the group's norms are accepted by a large majority of people. This process would find a correspondence in the relation of subjective and objective status. For example, Linton (46) states that where individuals are adjusted to their roles or statuses, society functions smoothly. Hence where a culture operates efficiently, there may be little discrepancy between subjective and objective status. Correspondingly, where there is great social change, there may be a large discrepancy between the two statuses. The process is probably reciprocal. Social change or social disorganization of necessity produces discrepancies between statuses since new roles are demanded, and such discrepancies are conducive to inefficiency and further change. During a period of marked social disorganization and change, the relation of subjective and objective status could be studied as in a post-war or revolutionary period.

There is one qualification: If subjective status may be conceived of as an adjustment to an undesirable objective status, the adjustment may operate to sterilize the resentment and desire for social change of those in unfortunate objective statuses. Hence a discrepancy may operate to lessen motivation for change. Such motivation, of course, will only produce change where repressive agents are not so strong as to prevent change. The American Dream represents a subjective (aspired) status which has mitigated the discontent of actual low status. There might be some threshold beyond which departure in status would lead to social disorganization. Another possible interpretation is that so long as the subjective status is not reflected in the person's behavior, it will not produce disorganization, *e.g.*, a workman may identify with or aspire for Henry Ford's status, but he does not go about acting like Henry Ford.

2. Implications for the Study of Race: The writer interviewed one Negro subject whose reference group for a variety of statuses included white persons. Inconsistencies in the operation of our class structure are striking in the case of Negroes. Mobility is valued and emphasized in the culture and denied to them in practice. This pattern may not impinge in the same way on all Negroes. When the reference group for status is a high status white group and mobility is denied, we have an inconsistent pattern that is highly operative at the personal level as in the case of this subject. If the inconsistency, however, does not operate at the personal level and the reference group is intra-racial or intra-class, there may be fewer unfortunate consequences. Sutherland (76) discusses these problems: The extent to which minority status is effective depends on the accommodations to inferior status, and the hopes of many Negro youths are defined by the culture of the Negro world itself. The imposition of a white reference group is probably a function of interaction with whites, and such interaction varies with the Negro's life situation.

An interesting suggestion about race and status may be found in Brenman's (7) work. In the above paragraph the suggestion was made that status comparisons might be intra-racial and that less discontent would follow. Yet Brenman notes that in the absence of extreme economic differences among urban northern Negroes, which differences exist in the white group with a consequently differentiated social scale, the felt necessity to establish socially distinct lines has been met by subtler scales. She lists seven determinants of status within the group which differentiate subclasses. Thus it seems that given the values and motives of a surrounding culture which stress mobility and enhancement of status, status distinctions may find avenues for development. Linton (46) has suggested that rigidly organized societies with no inter-class conflicts for status offer greater security. Similarly, Mead (54) has indicated a relation between cooperation in societies and social organization in which the individual's competition for status operates within small closed groups. Such security and cooperation may be offset, apparently, by intra-class competition providing there is some motor or "need" to develop status distinctions. It is true to some extent that such competition for status is attenuated by being isolated within class boundaries, but it may not be completely absent. Linton and Mead are probably correct in respect of two things. Rigidity of status provides security from outside competition for status. It also prevents any insecurity from fear of losing status, and it may produce cultural efficiency. However, no security or satisfactory life situation results to an individual of impoverished status just because his status cannot be changed. Furthermore, the writer has pointed out that intra-class competition for status may result.

3. Reference Groups and Satisfaction: The suggestion that stability and personal security are a function of fixity of status, intra-class goals, or intra-class reference groups has already been made. The theory derives some support from our data on the relation of aspiration and satisfaction. Where the discrepancy between aspirations and achievement was large, there was dissatisfaction. The data are reported in Chapter II, page 38. The use of an intra-class reference group may operate to lessen the difference between aspiration and achievement and also anchors the scale for judgment so as not to lower one's status markedly. Yet there is also contrary material on the problem: A. The American Dream has apparently operated to lessen the discontent of individuals. In this case there is a high reference group and dissatisfaction is not a consequence. B. There is the suggestion that if individuals of low status recognized their low status and their different possibilities, and lack of chance for betterment, there would be more discontent. This is contrary to the earlier relation between intra-class goals and satisfaction. C. Empirical interview data have been presented to indicate the wide use of reference groups and individuals of exceedingly high status who vicariously *enhance* the subject's status. D. Lewin, Lippit, and White (44) have suggested a positive correspondence between rigidity of group structure and aggression. How are these facts to be reconciled?

Several suggestions may be offered:

A. Reference Groups, classes and castes operate through the medium of individuals and a reference group may be manipulated in different ways to give different results. Two contrasted processes might be involved in the use of reference groups. There may be identification with the status of a high reference group. There may be the judgmental situation in which a high reference group or individual operates by stimulus anchoring or end anchoring to define the absolute scale. In the case of identification with a high reference group, there may be vicarious satisfaction. Correspondingly, identification with a low group and recognition of low status may cause dissatisfaction. Where the reference group operates as an anchoring agent, a high reference group produces low status and discontent, and a low reference group produces higher status and greater satisfaction. Hence, the process by which the variables are manipulated may hold the key to the consequences.

B. If we assume that the process is one of judgment in which a reference group or individual anchors the scale for the judgment of status, an alternative hypothesis may be suggested. Rogers (66) has shown that the degree of change in the scale when an additional anchoring agent (in this case a reference group) is introduced is a rectilinear function of the remoteness of the anchor. Beyond a certain degree of remoteness, however, the function breaks. This would mean with respect to status and the reference group that the use of an inter-class reference group might operate to lower the judgment of a person of low status up to a certain point. If the status of the reference group were very remote from the person's status (*e.g.*, if a share cropper used Henry Ford as a reference individual), there would be little additional loss in status.

C. The understanding of the phenomenon may not lie in the structure of class or caste societies per se, but in inconsistencies in their operation. A person who has a high status reference group in a society where there is actual mobility and a reasonable life chance of achieving higher status, may not manifest insecurity. Where there is in actuality no mobility and little realistic chance of achieving the higher status, there may be much insecurity. In this latter case it is necessary that the individual realize the impossibility of the aspiration. If mobility is unlikely and the individual, nevertheless, regards mobility as possible, as in the American Dream, the situation may not produce insecurity.

D. One might regard all such identification with high reference groups, the American Dream, manipulation of subjective status, etc. as overt reflections of a more basic insecurity which is characteristic of our class society. The writer has already pointed out that a high subjective status may provide satisfaction for individuals with low objective status, and that high reference groups offer vicarious status. Such phenomena lend credence to the suggestion that insecurity is characteristic of many individuals in our society.

Personality and the Psychology of Adjustment

1. The discrepancy between the objective status assigned an individual and his subjective status may be used as an indicator of the degree of adjustment of the individual to his life situation. Such

a discrepancy may be regarded as good or bad adjustment depending on one's norms as to the nature of adjustment. From the point of view of the individual, a discrepancy may aid adjustment. From the point of view of adjustment to the *realistic* life situation, a discrepancy between subjective and objective status may be regarded as an inadequate adjustment. Whisler and Remmers (82) suggest, "The study of individual and group morale by showing cases of undervaluation and of overvaluation can furnish a factual basis for constructive educational and social policy and add as well to social psychological theory." Linton's discussion of the incongruence of "status personality" and actual personality is analogous.

2. The interrelations between different statuses of an individual (objective or subjective) is an avenue to the psychology of adjustment. The plight of the academic man who has high social status and little economic status to support this social status is a case in point. Frank (19) suggests a study of the incongruities between the various ranks (of the individual) out of which problems of adjustment arise. He regards personality as the outcome of the individual's attempts to adjust to these incongruities.

3. Fantasy or autistic thinking may be partly understood in terms of status. Frank (19) remarks that for each status we may expect a set of beliefs through which the person will rationalize his rank. An objective status markedly removed from the mode or desirable status will stimulate rationalization. The individual may ignore ends of the status scale or reconstruct the status scale so as to manipulate or enhance his status (subjective).

4. Psychopathology may be conceived of as related to subjective status. A fantasy world may represent a situation in which an individual's status is enhanced or completely transformed. Sullivan (75) carries the conception farther. He suggests that the severity of any mental disorder is to an important degree a result of insecurity about one's status. This is true for our society where there is theoretical mobility of status as a function of the individual's own efforts. The possibility of change in status is important and actually valued, and an inadequacy is apt to handicap the individual's efforts to raise his status. Thus we have the vicious circle in which insecurity of status may produce maladjustment and such maladjustment then makes it more difficult to enhance status. Sullivan conceptualizes the mental hospital as a sort of caste society where there is no vertical mobility and hence little or no insecurity about status. It is improbable that status is a general etiological agent in mental disorder. In those cases, how-

ever, where status factors enter, the caste nature of the mental hospital provides freedom from insecurity about status.

Our norms of mental health may even be understood in part as a reflection of the formal mobility in our society. Davis (17) states, "Mental Hygiene unconsciously incorporates the open-class ethic." "Lack of ambition is felt to represent a definite symptom of maladjustment to be eliminated if possible." "The maladjusted person must learn to face reality, *i.e.*, the competitive facts." Such acceptance of the facts of mobility of status as norms for mental health conceals or neglects the very effect that status comparisons have in the production of psychopathology. Davis cites an (unpublished) analysis of 70 hospitalized cases reported in the literature in which all but 4 showed evidence of status involvement. He does not regard mental conflict as a function of class structure in itself but of inconsistency within the class structure, *e.g.*, theoretical mobility is permitted for all, but in practice mobility for Negroes and many other groups is denied.

Furthermore, the writer wishes to point out that inconsistency may operate not by a distinction between theory and practice but by the inconsistent operation of different status dimensions. Individuals may be given opportunity for mobility of intellectual status but not for economic or social status. Such a situation makes vivid to the person the possibility and desirability of enhancement of status in one respect but denies such opportunities in other respects. It might be argued that a basis for therapy would lie in the substitute satisfactions available in a milieu of multiple statuses. One could enhance one status and thereby compensate for another low immobile status. Such therapy to be effective would demand auxiliary principles. The statuses would have to be similarly valued initially or ultimately for one to operate in the place of another.

5. Certain problems of self-regard are amenable to clarification. Is a constant level of self-regard mirrored in one's judgments of specific statuses? Such does not seem to be the case, as is shown in Chapter V, Table 19. If the individual had some common level of self-regard, he might assign himself approximately the same status in different dimensions. Probably the degree of self-regard is best indicated in the individual's general status. Therefore, if the earlier analysis of general status is correct, this self-regard varies with the degree of importance attached to the specific statuses. Maslow (51) suggests approximately the same thing in discussing dominance-feeling when he states that the degree of importance of

a given attribute in the eyes of a person determines its import in his general dominance-feeling. Maslow reports that some women subjects who may have been low or average in dominance-feeling felt that they were superior in intellectual or mechanical or social ability. This is not the case because these factors are non-operative, but because in the composition of dominance, as in the case of general status, these variables are outweighed by other more valued ones.

JUDGMENT AND THE FRAME OF REFERENCE

The material on subjective status provides a situation in which certain principles of judgment may be extended to social problems. Analysis in terms of these principles has helped to clarify aspects of the problem of status. Further suggestions are offered below.

1. If reference groups operate to anchor the scale for the judgment of status, there is an available technique for experimental manipulation of status. One could enhance or lower the status of a subject by presenting reference groups relatively high or low in status. The question arises as to the permanence of such anchoring effects. An experiment on this problem should be designed.

2. In the field of anchoring it has been suggested that "specific objects or persons are much easier to conceptualize, to focus attention on, than are more general or complex . . ." (11). Reference groups varying in their specific character could be used to study this problem.

3. Problems of the frame of reference are amenable to analysis, e.g., the degree of departure of private status from objective status might vary inversely with the degree of structuration of the frame of reference; the lability of judgments of status might be an inverse function of degree of structuration The demonstration of such principles would further clarify problems of status. For example, the investigator would know how much experimental modification could be produced in various dimensions of status in terms of their relative structure. The writer, however, feels that such studies are equivocal unless the measure of degree of structuration, and the definition of the frame of reference are agreed upon. The term, frame of reference, is used in the literature to refer to objective factors in the field and internal frames which include preexisting attitudes, wishes, and knowledge. Variables such as ambiguity of the frame, and personal importance enter into the concept of structuration (10, 53). The concept of frame of reference cannot be dealt with rigorously when it subsumes the action of so many variables.

SUMMARY AND CONCLUSIONS

I. The discrepancy between the objective status of an individual and his subjective status has been indicated by a variety of studies. The need for an analysis of subjective status has been suggested by the writer, and a program of study has been completed.

II. A series of intensive interviews on a heterogeneous population of adults has demonstrated the action of variables such as the reference group, personal values, and criteria for the determination of status; all of these are essential to the understanding of subjective status.

III. Findings on the genesis of status, satisfaction with status, the function of status, and thoughts of status have been reported.

1. Status dimensions are precipitated by given kinds of experiences or limited by given stages of development.

2. Historically, status is specific.

3. Statuses operate with other variables to determine security feelings.

4. Striving for status is generally directed in the channel of the most valued status.

5. Statuses may be used as instrumentalities to achieve certain ends. When such instrumentalities are no longer needed, the dimension may vanish.

6. Dissatisfaction with status varies inversely with the level of status, providing there is high valuation of the status dimension.

7. Satisfaction with status is a function of aspiration for status.

8. Lack of concern with status may be associated with the similarity of the individual's status and the status of the reference group.

9. Lack of concern with status may be associated with a view which regards status differences as determined by a social order which is not acceptable to the subject.

10. Lack of concern with status may be a function of taking for granted one's superior status.

IV. A scale for the measurement of subjective status was constructed and the adequate reliability of the instrument has been demonstrated.

V. Variation of the reference group by instructions produces: A. Significant experimental shifts in status; B. Changes in the intercorrelation between dimensions of status; C. Changes in the reliability of judgments of status.

VI. The nature of general status and its composition has been studied. The findings suggest that general status represents a composite of specific statuses. The values of an individual are set into operation by certain reference groups, in which case specific statuses contribute to general status in accordance with their value.

VII. An analysis of the relation between economic radicalism and objective status as reported by various authors indicates that the relation in the majority of studies is equivocal. A study of economic radicalism and subjective status was therefore undertaken. The findings indicate a negligible relation, and reasons for the findings are offered.

VIII. Individuals who express dissatisfaction with their economic status are significantly more radical than individuals who express satisfaction.

IX. Suggestions have been presented for the future application of the concept of status to a variety of problems in social psychology and the field of personality.

BIBLIOGRAPHY

1. Allport, F. H. Social Psychology. Boston, Houghton, 1924.
2. Allport, G. W. The psychologist's frame of reference. Psychol. Bull., 1940, 37, 1–28.
3. Allport, G. W., and Vernon, P. E. A test for personal values. J. Abnorm. & Soc. Psychol., 1931, 26, 231–248.
4. American Institute of Public Opinion. (Released to the newspapers on April 2, 1939.)
5. Asch, S., Block, H., and Hertzman, M. Studies in the principles of judgments and attitudes: 1. Two basic principles of judgment. J. Psychol., 1938, 5, 219–251.
6. Bradshaw, F. F. The American Council on Education rating scale: its reliability, validity, and use. Arch. Psychol., 1930, 119.
7. Brenman, M. The relationship between minority-group membership and group identification in a group of urban middle class Negro girls. J. Soc. Psychol., 1940, 11, 171–197.
8. Breslaw, B. J. The development of a socio-economic attitude. Arch. Psychol., 1938, 226.
9. Cantril, H. General and specific attitudes. Psychol. Monog., 1932, 42, No. 5.
10. Cantril, H. The prediction of social events. J. Abnorm. & Soc. Psychol., 1938, 33, 364–389.
11. Cantril, H. The Psychology of Social Movements. New York, Wiley, 1941.
12. Cantril, H. Unpublished data on subjective class identification, 1941. Communicate with author.
13. Cantril, H., and Allport, G. W. Recent applications of the Study of Values. J. Abnorm. & Soc. Psychol., 1933, 28, 259–273.
14. Chapman, D., and Volkmann, J. A social determinant of the level of aspiration. J. Abnorm. & Soc. Psychol., 1939, 34, 225–238.
15. Cowdery, K. M. Measurement of professional attitudes. J. Person. Res., 1926, 5, 131–141.
16. Davis, A., and Dollard, J. Children of Bondage: The Personality Development of Negro Youth in the Urban South. Washington, American Council on Education, 1940.
17. Davis, K. Mental hygiene and the class structure. Psychiat., 1938, 1, 55–65.
18. Duffy, E., and Crissy, W. J. E. Evaluative attitudes as related to vocational interests and academic achievement. J. Abnorm. & Soc. Psychol., 1940, 35, 226–245.
19. Frank, L. K. Personality and rank order. Amer. J. Sociol., 1929, 35, 177–186.
20. Frazier, E. F. Negro Youth at the Crossways, Their Personality Development in the Middle States. Washington, American Council on Education, 1940.
21. Gumplowicz, L. The Outlines of Sociology. Philadelphia, American Academy of Political and Social Science, 1899.
22. Gundlach, R. H. Confusion among undergraduates in political and economic ideas. J. Abnorm. & Soc. Psychol., 1937, 32, 357–367.
23. Gundlach, R. H. Emotional stability and political opinions as related to age and income. J. Soc. Psychol., 1939, 10, 577–590.
24. Hall, O. M. Attitudes and unemployment. A comparison of the opinions, and attitudes of employed and unemployed men. Arch. Psychol., 1934, 165.
25. Harris, D. Group differences in "values" within a university. Psychol. Bull., 1933, 30, 555–556.
26. Harris, A. J., Remmers, H. H., and Ellison, C. E. The relation between liberal and conservative attitudes in college students, and other factors. J. Soc. Psychol., 1932, 3, 320–336.

27. Hartmann, G. W. The prestige of occupations. A comparison of educational occupations and others. Person. J., 1934, 13, 144–152.
28. Hartmann, G. W., and Newcomb, T. (editors). Industrial Conflict: A Psychological Interpretation. New York, Dryden Press, 1940, 195–198.
29. Hartshorne, H., and May, M. Studies in Deceit. New York, Macmillan, 1928.
30. Hertzman, M. Studies in the principles of judgments and attitudes: III. The functional equivalence of two differently structured references. J. Soc. Psychol., 1940, 12, 3–19.
31. Holcombe, A. N. The Middle Class in American Politics. Cambridge, Harvard University Press, 1940.
32. Hunt, J. McV., and Solomon, R. L. The stability and some correlates of group-status in a summer camp group of young boys. Amer. J. Psychol., 1942, 55, 33–46.
33. Hunt, W. A., and Volkmann, J. The anchoring of an affective scale. Amer. J. Psychol., 1937, 49, 88–92.
34. Johnson, C. S. Growing Up in the Black Belt; Negro Youth in the Rural South. Washington, American Council on Education, 1941.
35. Katz, D., and Cantril, H. Public opinion polls. Sociometry, 1937, 1, 155–179.
36. Kelly, T. Essential Traits of Mental Life. Cambridge, Harvard University Press, 1935.
37. Kerr, W. A., and Remmers, H. H. The construction and validation of a group home-environment scale. Psychol. Bull., 1941, 38, 705 (abstract).
38. Kornhauser, A. Analysis of ''class'' structure of contemporary American society—psychological bases of class divisions. In Psychology of Industrial Conflict, 1939, 199–265.
39. Kornhauser, A. Attitudes of economic groups. Publ. Opin. Quart., 1938, 2, 260–268.
40. Kornhauser, A. Reliability of average ratings. J. Person. Res., 1926, 5, 309–317.
41. Kornhauser, A. A study of social attitudes of individuals in relation to their economic position and personal desires. Psychol. Bull., 1937, 34, 707 (abstract).
42. Lentz, T. F. Personage admiration and other correlates of conservatism-radicalism. J. Soc. Psychol., 1939, 10, 81–93.
43. Lewin, K. Psycho-sociological problems of a minority group. Char. and Pers., 1935, 3, 175–187.
44. Lewin, K., Lippitt, R., and White, R. K. Patterns of aggressive behavior in experimentally created ''social climates.'' J. Soc. Psychol., 1939, 10, 271–299.
45. Linton, R. Age and sex in the social structure of non-literate societies. (Paper presented before Allied Social Science Associations, Dec. 27, 1941. Communicate with author.)
46. Linton, R. The Study of Man. New York, Appleton-Century, 1936.
47. Lundberg, G. A. Social attraction-patterns in a rural village: a preliminary report. Sociometry, 1937, 1, 77–80.
48. Lundberg, G. A. The demographic and economic basis of political radicalism and conservatism. Amer. J. Sociol., 1926–1927, 32, 719.
49. Lynd, R. Knowledge for What? Princeton, Princeton University Press, 1940.
50. Mallory, E. B. Father's occupation and boarding school education as related to the individual's judgment of values. Psychol. Bull., 1933, 30, 717 (abstract).
51. Maslow, A. H. Dominance feeling, behavior, and status. Psychol. Rev., 1937, 44, 404–429.
52. McCormick, M. J. Measuring social adequacy. Ment. Hyg., 1933, 17, 100–108.
53. McGregor, D. The major determinants of the prediction of social events. J. Abnorm. & Soc. Psychol., 1938, 33, 179–204.
54. Mead, M. Cooperation and Competition among Primitive Peoples. New York, McGraw, 1937.

55. Mintzer, S., and Sargent, S. S. The relationship between family economic status and some personality traits of college students. Sch. and Soc., 1939, 49, 322–324.
56. Mishkin, B. Rank and Warfare among the Plains Indians. American Ethnological Society, Monog., 1940, No. 3.
57. Murphy, G., and Likert, R. Public Opinion and the Individual. New York, Harper, 1938.
58. Murphy, G., Murphy, L., and Newcomb, T. Experimental Social Psychology. New York, Harper, 1937.
59. Newcomb, T., and Svehla, G. Intra-family relationships in attitude. Sociometry, 1937, 1, 180–205.
60. Newstetter, W., Feldstein, M., and Newcomb, T. Group Adjustment, A Study in Experimental Sociology. Cleveland, Western Reserve, 1938.
61. Pintner, R. A comparison of interests, abilities, and attitudes. J. Abnorm. & Soc. Psychol., 1933, 27, 351–357.
62. Quarterly Survey. Fortune, Jan. and Oct., 1936.
63. Radin, M. Status, in Encyclopedia of the Social Sciences. 1934, vol. 14, 373–377.
64. Reuter, E. B., and Hart, C. W. Introduction to Sociology. New York, McGraw, 1933.
65. Richardson, J. Law and Status among the Kiowa Indians. American Ethnological Society, Monog., 1940, No. 1.
66. Rogers, S. The anchoring of absolute judgments. Arch. Psychol., 1941, 261.
67. Roper, E. Classifying respondents by economic status. Publ. Opin. Quart., 1940, 4, 270–272.
68. Rosenthal, S. P. Change of socio-economic attitudes under radical motion picture propaganda. Arch. Psychol., 1934, 166.
69. Ross, E. A. Principles of Sociology. New York, Century, 1921.
70. Rundquist, E., and Sletto, R. Personality in the Depression. A Study in the Measurement of Attitudes. Minnesota, University of Minnesota Press, 1936.
71. Shen, E. The reliability coefficient of personal ratings. J. Educ. Psychol., 1926, 16, 232–236.
72. Sherif, M. The Psychology of Social Norms. New York, Harper, 1936.
73. Sims, V. M. Factors influencing attitude toward the TVA. J. Abnorm. & Soc. Psychol., 1938, 33, 34–56.
74. Sorokin, P. Leaders of labor and radical movements in the U. S. and foreign countries. Amer. J. Sociol., 1927, 33, 384–411.
75. Sullivan, H. S. Conceptions of modern psychiatry. Psychiat., 1940, 3, 1–117.
76. Sutherland, R. L. Color, Class, and Personality. Washington, American Council on Education, 1942.
77. Symonds, P. M. Diagnosing Personality and Conduct. New York, Century, 1931.
78. The people of the U. S. A.—a self-portrait. Fortune, Feb., 1940.
79. Vetter, G. B. The measurement of social and political attitudes and the related personality factors. J. Abnorm. & Soc. Psychol., 1930, 25, 149–189.
80. Volkmann, J. The anchoring of absolute scales. Psychol. Bull., 1936, 33, 742 (abstract).
81. Volkmann, J., Hunt, W. A., and McGourty, M. Variability of judgment as a function of stimulus-density. Amer. J. Psychol., 1940, 53, 277–284.
82. Whisler, L., and Remmers, H. H. A scale for measuring individual and group morale. J. Psychol., 1937, 4, 161–165.
83. Wilks, S. S. Representative sampling and poll reliability. Publ. Opin. Quart., 1940, 4, 259–269.
84. Willoughby, R. R. Liberalism, prosperity, and urbanization. J. Genet. Psychol., 1928, 35, 134–136.
85. Zeleny, L. D., Status: its measurement and control in education. Sociometry, 1941, 4, 193–204.

DISSERTATIONS ON SOCIOLOGY

An Arno Press Collection

Allison, Paul David. **Processes of Stratification in Science.** (Doctoral Dissertation, University of Wisconsin, 1976) 1980

Angell, Robert Cooley. **The Campus.** 1928

Bales, Robert Freed. **The "Fixation Factor" in Alcohol Addiction.** (Doctoral Dissertation, Harvard University, 1945) 1980

Barber, Bernard. **"Mass Apathy" and Voluntary Social Participation in the United States.** (Doctoral Dissertation, Harvard University) 1980

Beaver, Donald deB. **The American Scientific Community, 1800-1860.** (Doctoral Dissertation, Yale University, 1966) 1980

Becker, Howard S. **Role and Career Problems of the Chicago Public School Teacher.** (Doctoral Dissertation, University of Chicago, 1952) 1980

Birnbaum, Norman. **Social Structure and the German Reformation** (Doctoral Dissertation, Harvard University, 1957) 1980

Bittner, Egon. **Popular Interest in Psychiatric Remedies.** (Doctoral Dissertation, University of California, Los Angeles, 1961) 1980

Bredemeier, Harry C. **The Federal Public Housing Movement.** (Doctoral Dissertation, Columbia University, 1955) 1980

Breed, Warren. **The Newspaperman, News and Society** (Doctoral Dissertation, Columbia University, 1952) 1980

Caplovitz, David. **Student-Faculty Relations in Medical School** (Doctoral Dissertation, Columbia University, 1961) 1980

Clark, Burton R. **Adult Education in Transition.** 1956

Cohen, Steven Martin. **Interethnic Marriage and Friendship.** (Doctoral Dissertation, Columbia University, 1974) 1980

Cole, Stephen. **The Unionization of Teachers.** 1969

Costner, Herbert L. **The Changing Folkways of Parenthood.** (Doctoral Dissertation, Indiana University, 1960) 1980

Davis, Arthur K. **Thorstein Veblen's Social Theory.** (Doctoral Dissertation, Harvard University, 1941) With a New Foreword. 1980

Davis, Kingsley. **A Structural Analysis of Kinship.** (Doctoral Dissertation, Harvard University, 1936) 1980

Davison, W. Phillips. **The Berlin Blockade.** 1958

Devereux, Edward C., Jr. **Gambling and the Social Structure.** (Doctoral Dissertation, Harvard University, 1949) With a New Foreword. 1980

Duncan, Otis Dudley. **An Examination of the Problem of Optimum City Size.** (Doctoral Dissertation, University of Chicago, 1949) 1980

Elder, Glen H., Jr. **Family Structure and Socialization.** (Doctoral Dissertation, University of North Carolina, 1961) With a New Preface and Appendix Chapters. 1980

Etzioni, Amitai. **The Organizational Structure of the Kibbutz.** (Doctoral Dissertation, University of California, Berkeley, 1959) 1980

Friedman, Nathalie S. **Observability in School Systems.** (Doctoral Dissertation, Columbia University, 1968) 1980

Ginsberg, Ralph Bertram. **Anomie and Aspirations.** (Doctoral Dissertation, Columbia University, 1966) With a New Introduction and Appendix. 1980

Goode, Erich. **Social Class and Church Participation.** (Doctoral Dissertation, Columbia University, 1966) 1980

Goss, Mary E. Weber. **Physicians in Bureaucracy.** (Doctoral Dissertation, Columbia University, 1959) 1980

Hammond, Phillip Everett. **The Role of Ideology in Church Participation.** (Doctoral Dissertation, Columbia University, 1960) 1980

Hill, Robert Bernard. **Merton's Role Types and Paradigm of Deviance** (Doctoral Dissertation, Columbia University, 1969) 1980

Hyman, Herbert H. **The Psychology of Status.** (Doctoral Dissertation, Columbia University, 1942) 1942

Janowitz, Morris. **Mobility, Subjective Deprivation and Ethnic Hostility.** (Doctoral Dissertation, University of Chicago, 1948) 1980

Keller, Suzanne I. **The Social Origins and Career Lines of Three Generations of American Business Leaders.** (Doctoral Dissertation, Columbia University, 1953) 1980

Keyfitz, Nathan. **Urban Influence on Farm Family Size.** (Doctoral Dissertation, University of Chicago, 1952) 1980

Kohn, Melvin Lester. **Analysis of Situational Patterning in Intergroup Relations** (Doctoral Dissertation, Cornell University, 1952) 1980

Levine, Donald Nathan. **Simmel and Parsons.** (Doctoral Dissertation, University of Chicago, 1957) With a New Introduction. 1980

March, James G. **Autonomy as a Factor in Group Organization.** (Doctoral Dissertation, Yale University, 1953) With a New Introduction. 1980

Marsh, Robert M. **The Mandarins.** 1961

Moore, Wilbert E. **American Negro Slavery and Abolition.** 1971

Mullins, Nicholas C. **Social Networks among Biological Scientists** (Doctoral Dissertation, Harvard University, 1966) 1980

Nettler, Gwynne. **The Relationship between Attitude and Information Concerning the Japanese in America.** (Doctoral Dissertation, Stanford University, 1946) 1980

Nisbet, Robert A. **The Social Group in French Thought.** (Doctoral Dissertation, University of California, Berkeley, 1940) With a New Preface. 1980

O'Gorman, Hubert J. **Lawyers and Matrimonial Cases.** 1963

Reskin, Barbara F. **Sex Differences in the Professional Life Chances of Chemists.** (Doctoral Dissertation, University of Washington, 1973) With a New Introduction. 1980

Rosenberg, Morris. With the assistance of Edward A. Suchman and Rose K. Goldsen. **Occupations and Values.** 1957.

Rossi, Alice S. **Generational Differences in the Soviet Union.** (Doctoral Dissertation, Columbia University, 1957) 1980

Ryder, Norman B. **The Cohort Approach.** (Doctoral Dissertation, Princeton University, 1951) 1980

Schuessler, Karl F. **Musical Taste and Socio-Economic Background.** (Doctoral Dissertation, Indiana University, 1947) 1980

Short, James F., Jr. **An Investigation of the Relationship between Crime and Business Cycles.** (Doctoral Dissertation, University of Chicago, 1952) With a New Introduction. 1980

Sills, David L. **The Volunteers.** 1957.

Simmons, Roberta G. **An Experimental Study of the Role-Conflict of the First-Line Supervisor.** (Doctoral Dissertation, Columbia University, 1964) With a New Introduction. 1980

Skolnick, Jerome H. **The Stumbling Block.** (Doctoral Dissertation, Yale University, 1957) 1980

Storer, Norman W. **Science and Scientists in an Agricultural Research Organization.** (Doctoral Dissertation, Cornell University, 1961) 1980

Stouffer, Samuel A. **An Experimental Comparison of Statistical and Case History Methods of Attitude Research** (Doctoral Dissertation, University of Chicago, 1930) 1980

Strodtbeck, Fred L. **A Study of Husband-Wife Interaction in Three Cultures.** (Doctoral Dissertation, Harvard University, 1950) 1980

Swanson, Guy E. **Emotional Disturbance and Juvenile Delinquency** (Doctoral Dissertation, University of Chicago, 1948) 1980

Thielens, Wagner P., Jr. **The Socialization of Law Students.** (Doctoral Dissertation, Columbia University, 1965) 1980

Trow, Martin A. **Right-Wing Radicalism and Political Intolerance.** (Doctoral Dissertation, Columbia University, 1957) 1980

Vidich, Arthur J. **The Political Impact of Colonial Administration.** (Doctoral Dissertation, Harvard University, 1953) 1980

White, Harrison C. **Research and Development as a Pattern in Industrial Management.** (Doctoral Dissertation, Princeton University, 1960) 1980

Wright, Charles R. **The Effect of Training in Social Research on the Development of Professional Attitudes.** (Doctoral Dissertation, Columbia University, 1954) 1980

Wrong, Dennis H. **Class Fertility Trends in Western Nations.** (Doctoral Dissertation, Columbia University, 1956) 1980

Yinger, J. Milton. **Religion in the Struggle for Power.** 1946.